CLASSROOM VIBE

PRAISE FOR *CLASSROOM VIBE*

What we need in our career, whether we are at the beginning, middle or end, is a partner in learning who inspires us to become more curious about what we do because they are curious about what they do. Tim does that in *Classroom Vibe*.

Peter DeWitt, leadership coach, author
and Education Week blogger

Classroom Vibe is a superb read for educators new and experienced alike. O'Leary offers a clear guide for teachers to identify the impact they are having on students' learning and encouragement to ensure their practice is student-centred and learning driven. Teachers will find affirmation of their own effective practices while also reflecting deeply on what they can do to improve the culture in their classroom.

James Nottingham, keynote speaker,
company director and author of 11 books

Tim O'Leary provides an honest, well-written, and thoughtful account of teaching accompanied by practical strategies that will equip classroom teachers with the tools they need to be successful. Readers will find a wealth of ideas and resources that can be applied in practice with relative ease. A very enjoyable read.

Jenni Donohoo, five-time best-selling author
and professional learning facilitator

The personal narrative style and humble tone make it really readable and accessible. The reader doesn't feel as though they are being told what to do or what to think – rather he/she is invited to reflect on their own lived experiences to identify how they can engage with the ongoing process of learning and growth. I love the summaries and reflective questions at the end of the chapter – it presents almost like a reflective handbook/journal for teachers.

Jacqui Coker, Director of Professional Learning

Classroom Vibe is an intelligent, well-researched boot camp of a book. It takes teachers and leaders on the journey from novice to expert highlighting the crucial steps along the way. Very much inspired by the likes of Hattie, Marzano and Robinson it seeks to switch the dial from emphasis on teaching to emphasis on learning.

Stephen Cox, CEO and educational leader

CLASSROOM VIBE

TIMOTHY M. O'LEARY, PH.D.

Copyright © Timothy M. O'Leary 2021

All rights reserved. No part of this book may be reproduced or transmitted in any form or by any means, electronic or mechanical, including photocopying, recording or by any information storage and retrieval system, without prior permission in writing from the publisher.

Published by Amba Press
Melbourne, Australia
www.ambapress.com.au

Editor – Pauline Hopkins
Cover Designer – Alissa Dinallo
Illustrations – Kate McKinnon

Printed by IngramSpark

ISBN: 9781922607102 (pbk)
ISBN: 9781922607119 (ebk)

A catalogue record for this book is available from the National Library of Australia.

For Nick, Branko, Anne, Richard, Linda, Jacqui, and countless others. Thank you for challenging and supporting me to be a better teacher.

To my students past and present. Thank you for your patience as I learn to be better.

Contents

Contents	ix
Figures	x
Tables	xi
Foreword	xiii
About the Author	xvii
Acknowledgements	xviii
Preface – What to Do with a Dream	xix
Introduction	1
Chapter 1 – It's the Vibe	11
Chapter 2 – Nurturing Classroom Vibe	29
Chapter 3 – Enhancing Teacher Credibility	49
Chapter 4 – Enhancing Teacher Clarity	77
Chapter 5 – Considerations for Leaders	111
So, What Next?	121
Chapter Notes	125
References and Suggested Readings	127
Appendices	135

Figures

Figure 1.	What are the Sources of Variation on Student Achievement?	12
Figure 2.	How Do Student Perceptions about Trusting Relationships Vary?	17
Figure 3.	Student Perceptions of Teaching of Four Example Classes	18
Figure 4.	Variation in Student Perceptions Within and Between Classes	18
Figure 5.	Teacher Credibility + Teacher Clarity = A Classroom with Vibe	25
Figure 6.	The Classroom Vibe Theory of Change	25
Figure 7.	Classroom Vibe Inquiry Cycle	30
Figure 8.	Amplifying Improvement with Feedback	43
Figure 9.	Amplifying Improvement with Feedback	46
Figure 10.	The Building Blocks of Teacher Credibility	49
Figure 11.	Steps to Maximising Academic Learning Time in Class	69
Figure 12.	The Building Blocks of Teacher Clarity	77
Figure 13.	Finding Flow	84
Figure 14.	Decrease of Recall Over Time	86
Figure 15.	Example K-W-L + S Chart	106
Figure 16.	Influences on Student Learning	112
Figure 17.	Self Determination Theory	114
Figure 18.	Continuum of Motivation	115
Figure 19.	Enabling Conditions for Collective Teacher Efficacy	116

Tables

Table 1.	Examples of High Impact Teaching Strategies	13
Table 2.	High Impact Teaching Strategies Related to Classroom Climate	21
Table 3.	High Impact Influences within Teacher Credibility and Teacher Clarity	22
Table 4.	Classroom Vibe – Self-Assessment Rubric	33
Table 5.	Micro-Teaching & Observation Assessment Rubric	35
Table 6.	Sample Student Perception of Teaching Questions	36
Table 7.	Smart Goals Setting Unpacked	39
Table 8.	Classroom Vibe Goal Setting Template	41
Table 9.	Planning for Success Template	42
Table 10.	Proposed Implementation of Classroom Vibe Inquiry Cycle	45
Table 11.	Further Examples of Interactive Teaching Strategies	68
Table 12.	Example Learning Intentions	82
Table 13.	Product vs Process Success Criteria	83
Appendix 1.	Classroom Vibe – Self-Assessment Rubric	136
Appendix 2.	Classroom Vibe – Micro-Teaching & Observation Assessment Rubric	137
Appendix 3.	Sample Student Perception of Teaching Questions	138
Appendix 4.	Classroom Vibe Goal Setting Template	139
Appendix 5.	Planning for Success Template	140
Appendix 6.	Proposed Implementation of Classroom Vibe Inquiry Cycle	141

Foreword

EMERITUS LAUREATE PROFESSOR JOHN HATTIE

In the 1997 film *The Castle*, the now legendary but fictitious lawyer Dennis Denuto was flummoxed and realised he had no argument when he summed up his case to the High Court Judge. So his retort, when asked what section of the Constitution was being violated, was "There is no one section, it's just the vibe of the thing … In summing up it's the constitution, it's Mabo, it's justice, it's law, it's the vibe and, no that's it, it's the vibe. I rest my case." Students know the vibe as they walk into a class, and teachers know the vibe when they walk into a school. Yes, we have fancier words — culture, climate, mood — but this book's title captures the feeling of classrooms and staffrooms. Grounded in evidence, resplendent in actionable takeaways, the fundamental message is about establishing a vibe, ensuring the students feel it and want to be part of it, and that there is a joy in teaching and learning.

Along with my colleagues, I completed a study of what adults recalled about their best teachers (Clinton et al., 2018). Two features dominated: either the teacher wanted to turn them onto the teacher's passion, and/or the teacher saw something more in the student than they did themselves. Passion for their subjects and high expectations of their students are the common denominators of memorable teachers. When we recall the bad teachers, the common refrain is that they were unfair, did not care if we learnt or not, and had no vibe. Those teachers who fell somewhere in the middle between those two camps may be okay, we may learn, but without the vibe, we are likely to lack recall of these teachers. We all have a gallery of the famous, the infamous, and the forgettable.

So how to create the right vibe – felt by all, but hard to deconstruct. This is what this book is about — the deconstruction of the essence of memorable classrooms. It starts with teachers enjoying working with young people – oh, do the students feel that very quickly. And if the teacher loses the love over time, then learning in their classes becomes routine, boring, dominated by teacher talk, instructions, surveillance, and boredom.

Same in the staffroom. The research on teacher attrition shows that most teachers do not leave because of the students, but they do leave because of their colleagues. The vibe in the staffroom is core to decisions to stay or leave the profession, and we need to ask why some staffroom vibes lead to the boring, the tired, and the ineffectual to remain in the profession. Hence the importance of the vibe created by the school leaders.

A core claim by Timothy O'Leary is that a healthy vibe is a function of improvement. If the students believe they are improving, if the teachers believe they are improving, if the school leaders believe they are improving, you have a healthy, flourishing, and welcoming school. If we are not improving or committed to improvement, then we are in a rut – and this is obvious, felt, and not enjoyed by many.

But O'Leary does not make the mistake of providing tips and tricks or something you can do tomorrow, but goes to the core of improvement and creating the vibe – the belief systems of the educators. How many times have we all seen high probability and research-rich ideas introduced into a school to see them fall flat? The students know almost instinctively that the beliefs and biases of the teacher are more important than what they say; and those students who do not know this are typically pathologized as the naughty and ill-disciplined. Understanding a teacher's theory of action is the essence for then implementing improvements; start there and all good can follow.

The author's argument is "that a razor-sharp focus on improving each teacher's classroom vibe will yield teachers focused on improving what we know will enhance student learning" (page 6). So what are the teachers' beliefs about their vibe, their theories of action? He centres their beliefs around two powerful notions: credibility and clarity.

Credibility includes presence, impact, trusting relationships, competence, and passion – all detectable in the class by students, and in the staffroom by teachers. We all know classes where there are low expectations for all, where some peers are deliberately left behind or given low quality tasks, where there is low trust not only with the teacher but between students, where competitiveness surmounts cooperation, where there is all talk and no listening, and where inclusion and equity are absent. Students are brilliant vibe-detectors (as are teachers in staffrooms).

Clarity includes being specific about when 'good is good enough', about where each student is now and where they need to be, making clear the 'why' of the learning, and teaching to reduce this gap, about how to build confidence that the success is achievable (with help), about how to welcome errors and not knowing as opportunities for learning (not unwelcome interlopers), knowing the balance of content and depth of thinking in the teaching, ensuring every student is appropriately challenged, as well as being fair, firm, on time, and predictable in your reactions. He regards assessment as the opportunity to illustrate clarity in purpose, improvement, and success, and not as the usual 'stick' to cajole students to engage. Students detect a teacher's passion to improve them, and the aim, claims O'Leary, is to be infectious in this pursuit of improvement and illuminate the path to success.

His section on collective teacher efficacy could just as easily be translated into student collective efficacy (Hattie et al., 2021) – simply replace school leaders to teachers with teachers to students. The claim is that school leaders should start and continually harness the potential impact of their teachers by focusing on building the culture within their school such that their teachers are effectively empowered to understand and enhance the vibe in each of their classrooms. They "must focus their work, their improvement efforts on creating systems, structures, and processes to support and empower their teachers to make changes to improve their practice by focusing on their classroom vibe" (page 113).

As I ponder the big ideas in this book, it speaks to my most enjoyable role as an academic – supervising thesis students. They pay to come to graduate school, become immersed in their passion, teach me details and ideas from their depth of reading literature, push me to question my assumptions, theories of action, and interpretations – and I get paid to do this! Tim was one of the 200+ thesis students who lived the vibe of discovery, put in the hard work to then bounce in with new ideas, new articles, new interpretations. His work on how to report scores from tests so they are interpretable broke new ground, and he was continually amazed with new discoveries, excited about meeting his gurus, engaged deeply in discussion and debate, and he still continues this growth. His vibe is passion, communication, sharing, and 'figuring it out'; and this first book is a testament to these attributes. May there be many more. "Don't worry about it, Mr O'Leary. It's okay. It was high school. Back then, we were all figuring stuff out" (Page 2).

REFERENCES

Clinton, J. M., Hattie, J. A. C. and Nawab, D. (2018). The good teacher: Our best teachers are inspired, influential and passionate. pp. 880-889 in M. Harring (Ed.). *Handbook for School Pedagogics*. Munster, Germany: Waxmann.

Hattie, J. A. C., Clarke, S., Fisher, D. and Frey, N. (2021). *Collective Student Efficacy*. Thousand Oaks, CA: Corwin.

About the Author

Timothy M. O'Leary, Ph.D., is the Managing Director of Educational Data Talks, an education consulting company focused on supporting educators to engage with data through tailored professional development, leadership development, monitoring and evaluation, and research. Tim is also an Honorary Fellow and Adjunct Lecturer at The University of Melbourne, doing ongoing research and work with Professor John Hattie and teaching Master of Teaching students about the joy of developmental approaches to teaching and learning. Tim is a father of three and a self-professed data aficionado or nerd (depending on your perspective). Tim began his career as a land surveyor, worked as an IT Consultant, and qualified as a teacher after realising the error of his ways. As an educator, Tim has worked in government, independent, and faith-based schools. He has worked across a variety of settings, including school, vocational, tertiary, and consultancy. Within schools, Tim's roles have ranged from classroom teacher to school leader; his most recent role was as Director of Learning at an inner-city P-12 school in Australia. Tim's greatest professional love is working with people, supporting them to use evidence to drive school improvement. He has coached and mentored Principals, Deputy Principals, and mid- and senior-level school leaders across a range of schools in the effective use of various forms of data to evaluate school impact and identify opportunities for celebration and improvement. Tim has published on data interpretation and analysis, effective score reporting, and collective teacher efficacy. He is also obsessively interested in the use of student perceptions of teaching to inform personalised teacher professional development.

Acknowledgements

This is my first book. Without the encouragement, love, and friendship of a great many people, it may never have come to be. As such, there are several people to thank.

First, I would like to thank my colleague Anna Dabrowski who has been telling me to capture my thinking about this idea for nearly five years. Thank you for pushing me to get started and helping me to finish.

Next, I would like to thank John Hattie, my friend and mentor. You guided me through my postgraduate work and have, once again, patiently turned your intellect to provide insights that have improved the quality of my story.

Third, I would like to thank my friends and colleagues Dr Peter DeWitt, Dr Jenni Donohoo, Ilja Van Weringh and Georgia Heffernan. Each of you has given up time to provide feedback on drafts of this book which has only made it better and me richer for the experience. Thank you!

I would like to also thank Alicia Cohen of Amba Press for taking this idea from me, an unknown, untested author, and helping make my book a reality. Thank you.

And finally, to my wife Louise, and three children Harry, Emily, and Dawson. It is a big thing to write a book. And an even bigger thing to make space in your life for someone to write one. Thank you for your support through this journey and for allowing me the time I have needed to spend on this task. I appreciate it and love you more for it. I promise I won't start the next book too soon. Maybe. Actually, I have already begun. But that's why I love you, and that's why we work.

Preface – What to Do with a Dream

Writing this book has been a labour of both love and frustration.

To be honest, I never thought that I had a book in me. I honestly didn't know I had anything to say. Once I realised there was one, though, I ignored it. I found reason after reason to delay for as long as I could.

Eventually, I began. It was daunting, and I never thought I would quite get there.

Despite this, once I got going, once I found my rhythm, the words came quickly. Now that the book is written, I am content. I have found my voice.

One of the reasons I wrote this book is because, in all honesty, at the beginning of my career, I felt wholly unprepared to be a teacher. I was, of course, a 'qualified' mathematics teacher. With a land surveying degree, there is no doubt I knew my subject matter. But given the length of a Graduate Diploma of Education and the minimal classroom experience one really gains, I only had an inkling of what it was to be a teacher. I had done teaching rounds, of course, but teaching one or two classes for a few weeks at a time, under supervision, is entirely different from having five classes of your own.

Further to this, my first teaching role was in what was designated a hard-to-staff school. It was a low socioeconomic status school with a truly diverse population in terms of ethnicity, language background, behavioural issues, and developmental readiness to learn. It was almost overwhelming. Don't get me wrong, the kids were wonderful and energising, but for me, this was not a great place to start my teaching career. I spent a lot of my time learning, often unsuccessfully, to manage poor classroom behaviour. It was almost the end for me.

Fortunately, I had the opportunity to transition early in my career to a suburban school—a place where I had more of an opportunity to hone my teaching practice. I made mistakes, of course. But thanks to several mentors along the way, and the opportunities I had for professional learning and post-graduate study, I had the chance to improve.

This book has been my opportunity to share my thinking about what helped me become a better teacher. The things I wish I had learned much earlier. I hope that this book may give other teachers some ideas and shortcuts to improve their practice.

I genuinely hope that you enjoyed reading this book. I also hope that it challenges your thinking, causes you to reflect on your practice and inspires you to be even better tomorrow than you are today.

Thank you for reading!

Introduction

I never planned to become a teacher. Like most of the good things that have happened in my life, it happened by lucky accident. When I was at school, most of my peers already had a strong sense of what they wanted to be when they grew up. I did not. While I enjoyed learning, I had no direction.

Mind you, given I have spent most of my adult life working in schools, I have perhaps been saved from the embarrassment of needing to know what I wanted to be when I left school.

Given this firm foundation, post-school, I quite literally drifted along. My career was much more the verb than the noun. First, I completed a double degree focused on engineering (land surveying) and science (geography). Then I worked variously as an IT consultant, casual martial arts instructor, vocational education lecturer, and mathematics tutor, to name but a sample of my chequered employment history.

Life was most certainly fun. It just lacked direction.

It was not until much later that I realised what should have been obvious. The common feature of the work I enjoyed most was teaching. The greatest pleasure I experienced in my work until then was in supporting others with their learning. This realisation was the crystallising moment when my true vocation, education, emerged.

This realisation did not mean that learning to be a teacher was easy for me. From the outset, I suffered from the belief that being a good teacher meant knowing my subject matter and covering the prescribed curriculum. At the time, I believed that if I knew my material and delivered the curriculum, my students would learn, and then I would be a respected teacher. I would be a success; life would be good.

Boy, was I wrong! In the hope that it will help others, I will happily admit now that I struggled. My over-reliance on subject matter expertise and the assumption that this would result in effective classroom practice meant that teaching felt like more of a battle than it should have. Sadly, I do not doubt that many of my students probably felt the same.

Looking back with the benefit of hindsight, I see now that one of the main things I failed to do was to focus on building the culture in my classrooms. The atmosphere I nurtured was wrong. It was not learning-focused. It was teaching-focused. My students perceived this, and my classroom culture, the 'vibe', suffered.

Occasionally, when I reflect on this, I sometimes feel a deep shame that I did not know then what I know now. Perhaps I might have taken a different approach. Maybe I would have cultivated better relationships and cultures in my classrooms. Would I have then had an even more significant impact on the lives of those students who have passed through my classrooms? I do not lose sleep over this by any means, but there is undoubtedly regret. Several years ago, I had the good fortune of meeting a past student and sharing my embarrassment. His response both disarmed and inspired me to be a little forgiving of myself. They said, and I paraphrase, "Don't worry about it, Mr O'Leary. It's okay. It was high school. Back then, we were all figuring stuff out." Isn't that the truth? His comments almost brought a tear to my eye. They still do. Almost.

Fortunately, since early in my career, I have had the support and guidance of many great teachers who have helped me to reframe my beliefs and subsequent actions. Over time, this support resulted in a transformation in my approach to teaching. I shifted from teaching the curriculum to teaching my students. For their help, I am eternally grateful. My life has been all the richer.

In many ways, this book is a testament to the support and guidance they have provided me and, hopefully, a roadmap for other teachers to help them learn from my mistakes.

SO WHAT DRIVES SOMEONE TO BECOME A TEACHER?

Teaching is a challenging profession. On any day, a teacher can feel they are suffering from a multiple personality disorder as they switch between various identities to support their students. It is certainly not a career for the faint-hearted, nor a career for someone without passion. Indeed, I have met many teachers and, as best as I can tell, no one becomes a teacher to do a lousy job.

Of course, teachers are at different stages in their careers and there might be those who are stuck in a rut. Or even those with varying points of view about what good teaching involves. As best as I can see, though, there is no evidence that people are attracted to teaching for disreputable reasons. In fact, in support of this, a 2015 survey of trainee and newly qualified teachers[1] in the UK highlighted some of the main reasons people have chosen to become teachers:

Enjoy working with young people (81%)
To make a difference (75%)
Inspired by my teacher(s) at school (38%)
Love of subject (36%)
Teaching is fun (32%)
Great experience in my own education (30%)

These findings align with evidence from a much broader study[2] involving 20,000 US public school teachers that found key positive reasons, including:

To make a difference in the lives of children (85%)
To share their love of learning (74%)
To help students reach their full potential (71%)
To be a part of those 'aha' moments (66%)
Because a teacher inspired them when they were young (50%)

IMPROVEMENT — THE GREAT CHALLENGE IN EDUCATION!

As you can see, no one becomes a teacher to do a poor job! Despite this, though, no matter their underlying motivation, every teacher can improve. Wherever they are in their career, beginning, middle or end, a teacher always has the opportunity to hone their capacity and capability in the classroom. To get better at what they do. To improve their ability to impact student learning in a positive way. This point is essentially what this book is about: encouraging teachers to understand and seek to improve their practice in service of their students.

The thing is, though, improvement is often hard in education. Having been a teacher and school leader for almost two decades, I believe there are several reasons for the inevitable challenge of change.

The first is the consequence of how an individual's personal beliefs, values, and motivations, combined with their underlying cognitive biases, can impact their capacity to change. Fundamental to this is the notion of theory of action or change. Put simply, a theory of action or change is a logical chain of reasoning which explains how change or action occurs. Theories of action can be helpful to use, as they highlight how an action or change should impact practice and result in the desired outcome or, in this instance, how an individual teacher perceives and enacts their role. The point is that no matter how good a proposed improvement initiative might be, it can be almost impossible for a teacher to change when their theory of action, values, and beliefs conflict with or stand in contradiction to it. For example, it can be challenging to shift teacher practice with regards to differentiating practice to meet the needs of the diverse range of students in their classroom if they firmly believe it is their job to deliver the documented curriculum; this was one of my initial challenges when beginning my career. Deep down, I knew I wasn't meeting the needs of all my students, but I felt pressure, from who knows where, to push on with the designated curriculum. Professor Viviane Robinson's book *Reduce Change to Increase Improvement* is an excellent book for a deeper understanding of this point.

Secondly, there is a long list of things we know that are effective teaching practices, and it can be pretty confusing if not overwhelming to know where to start. For example, John Hattie's evolving *Visible Learning* research and Robert Marzano's *The Art and Science of Teaching* are two seminal bodies of work that have influenced our understanding of what works in education. They have also created a more mainstream discussion about the impact of what teachers do in the classroom. Now, don't get me wrong; they are great resources, but, as I said, knowing where to start for a teacher is almost crippling.

Thirdly, and linked to the previous two points, there is a plethora of professional learning made available to and enacted upon teachers. Despite this, a 2015 study by The New Teacher Project (TNTP, 2015) which explored teacher professional development, found that despite significant investment in teacher development, there was little evidence of improvement in teacher practice and, when there were improvements, it was often not the result of professional development efforts. Further, the research demonstrated that despite various systems to support teacher professional development, they were not helping teachers understand that there was room for improvement in their practice and, more importantly, how to achieve this improvement (TNTP, 2015). The researchers found that most of the teachers in the study were rated as 'Meeting Expectations' or above despite clear capacity for improvement in student learning outcomes. Worse still, of the teachers who were rated poorly, there was strong evidence of a perception-reality gap with more than 60% rating themselves as high performance. This disparity is an excellent example of illusory superiority, a form of cognitive bias that we will discuss in greater detail shortly. The TNTP further lamented that "teachers need clear information about their strengths and weaknesses to improve their instruction, but many don't seem to be getting that information" (p. 2).

An important question moving forward is how do we provide such evidence? We will address this question later in the book.

Finally, pressure from school leadership or education systems can present a confusing landscape for teachers. Teachers can often feel pushed and pulled in a myriad of seemingly competing directions which often change annually. The result is overburdened, under-resourced teachers wanting to do a good job but on the fast track to feeling inundated with change. If I think back to my work in schools, I was asked countless times to improve and implement many more strategies than I can remember. See below for a small selection to name a few:

- Feedback
- Formative Assessment
- Growth Mindset
- Concept-based Learning
- Student Wellbeing
- Metacognition
- Learning Intentions & Success Criteria
- Inquiry
- Student Voice/Agency

I am curious. Do any of these initiatives sound familiar to you? The research literature no doubt provides a great deal of evidence as to their potential for impact. Unfortunately, I can say with great certainty that I have never actually seen these strategies implemented well or, at least, achieve their potential for impact on student learning.

I do not believe this lack of impact was due to a lack of motivation or desire by those teachers asked to improve. Instead, in my view, the processes of implementation I experienced were disjointed and unnecessarily complex. They felt like they focused on implementing disparate strategies (often concurrently and in rapid-fire). Worse still, they often seemed to focus on changes a teacher needed to make to their teaching or what a teacher was supposed to learn instead of how their students experienced these changes as learners in the classroom. The problem with this is, no matter how much we 'change' as teachers in terms of what we know, if it is in isolation to or does not manifest in our classrooms, through the learning-focused atmosphere we cultivate, what I call a classroom's 'vibe', then we miss the point.

In my view, the atmosphere, the classroom vibe experienced by our students should be the area of focus for analysis and improvement. Yes, the strategies are important, but they must be embedded where the learning happens.

This book is my attempt to cut through the confusion I believe is present. It is my way of simplifying the improvement process for teachers and helping school leaders see and use a more holistic approach to their leadership and school improvement efforts.

I hope to achieve this by presenting a framework that highlights how the culture of a classroom, its 'vibe', can integrate high-impact teaching strategies; this is to provide teachers a singular focus for their improvement efforts, the 'vibe' in each of their classrooms. And further still, to offer school leaders a framework within which they can focus their efforts on supporting their teachers. Essentially, my argument is that a razor-sharp focus on improving each teacher's classroom vibe will yield teachers focused on improving what we know will enhance student learning.

MAKING THE MOST OF THIS BOOK

I have written this book to support teachers to reflect on and improve their practice. I have discussed research when necessary, but my focus is on providing strategies to enhance classroom vibe. I have cited when necessary, and I have included a comprehensive list of readings and references at the conclusion of the book.

As you read this book and engage with the learning, it is essential to pause and reflect on the ideas and their implication for your practice. To support this, I have included questions to help guide your reflection. There are four reasons I have included these questions. Firstly, because in the busyness of our work in school, it can sometimes be hard to find the space to take a few moments and think – I hope reading this book helps you create some space. Secondly, to provide some structure to help you review the ideas and strategies introduced throughout each chapter and to help you integrate them into your thinking. Third, to help you reflect on your current practice and perhaps consider your classroom practice through a different lens. And, finally, to help you plan for how you might integrate some of the new ideas into your practice in the future.

In this book, I will introduce a variety of ideas and strategies. Some of these will be new, some you will already know. As you read, please remember it is human nature to have your own views about these in terms of their effectiveness and your capability and capacity to implement them. These views are relevant, but it is important to recognise they can be affected by cognitive biases, which can impede our ability to engage objectively with data, evidence, and ideas. To be afflicted by these types of biases is human nature too and can, in many instances, help us, but sometimes it means we can miss opportunities to improve by dismissing them too readily. To ensure that you get the most out of this, I would like to take a moment to remind you of three powerful cognitive biases that can affect our judgment – I should know as I fallen victim to each of these on many occasions.

Confirmation Bias

Confirmation bias relates to the tendency to search for, interpret, prefer, or recall information and details that confirm our existing beliefs. Confirmation bias can be a particularly tricky bias as it means that we can often miss or unintentionally ignore critical information that might serve as a powerful disconfirmation of our perceived reality.

Illusory Superiority Bias

Illusory superiority bias is a tendency for people to overestimate their personal qualities and abilities in comparison to the same qualities and abilities in other people – think Donald Trump (please excuse my obvious politics). A classic example of illusory superiority comes from a study of a teaching faculty at the University of Nebraska during the 1970s (see Cross, 1977). A questionnaire was compiled and distributed to university faculty members to gain insights into their perceptions regarding their teaching proficiency. The resulting data captured 29% of the teaching population across the university's three sites. Analysis of the results showed that 94% of the respondents rated themselves as above average. Further, 68% considered themselves in the top 25% of teachers. Pretty interesting, right? Other researchers have shown similar findings in professors at other universities such as Stanford. Additionally, research has shown comparable results in other human endeavours, including perceptions about driving ability and health and health-related behaviour. When writing this book, I ran a LinkedIn poll asking teachers, "How do you rate yourself as a teacher?" Response options were: Above Average, About Average or Below Average. My sample size was smaller than the studies mentioned, but my results were similar, showing that 50% of teachers considered themselves above average and 97% 'about average' or 'above average.' Scary stuff. No wonder it can be difficult to convince teachers there is a need for improvement.

Status Quo Bias

This bias is a preference for people to want things to stay the same, despite the fact that evidence may strongly support change (think smokers) or that the changes could potentially lead to significant benefits. This bias makes me think of the quote credited to pioneering American computer scientist and US Navy Rear Admiral Grace Hopper:

> *The most dangerous phrase in the language is 'we've always done it this way'.*

I have heard this expression, or versions of it, many times in the schools in which I have worked. It has been a little soul-destroying each time.

The purpose of spending time thinking about these cognitive biases is that we, as fallible individuals, need to be mindful of ourselves. As such, as you read this book, you are gently challenged to:
1. Be open to examining ideas and thinking about how they confirm or challenge your existing beliefs and inform your future actions.
2. Take a moment to pause and reflect when you find yourself critical or dismissive of new ideas. Consider what is driving your reaction and ask yourself: do I have evidence to support my feelings? If not, think about what sort of objective evidence you might need to confirm or disconfirm your current belief and change your behaviours. Do you need to read some contemporary research or seek feedback from your peers or students?
3. Actively, unapologetically, seek to make changes when presented with evidence supporting new strategies that will improve your teaching, even when they make you feel uncomfortable.

THESE EFFECT SIZES ARE MAKING ME CRAZY

If you work in education and have not heard of effect size, you must have been living under a rock! Throughout this book, I reference what I call known high-impact strategies. I use the word 'known' because past research has shown them to be effective – though I should caution that past research is not always a good indicator of the future or what is appropriate in your particular context. In talking about these strategies, I sometimes refer to effect sizes because, well, that is what you do in education.

But what exactly is an effect size?

Put simply, an effect size is a measure for quantifying the magnitude of an observed difference or relationship. For instance, if you are interested in understanding the impact of a new reading comprehension program, you might conduct an experiment to compare the difference in student achievement between two randomly assigned groups of students, one assigned to the existing program and one to the new program. In this case, you would calculate an effect size to quantify the difference between the groups, allowing you to make inferences about the program's effectiveness.

In academic research, effect sizes are important. In quantitative research (i.e., research where you measure things) they are required – I learned this the hard way when trying to get a paper published during my Ph.D. This requirement is because it is not only important whether an observed difference or relationship or effect is likely to have happened. What is more valuable is knowledge of how large the effect is. This is because while an observed effect might be statistically significant, the actual size of the effect might be negligible. On the other hand, an observed effect might not be statistically meaningful, but it might be big enough to be interesting and warrant further consideration.

While the phrase 'effect size' is increasingly used in education, we need to be mindful that there are different types of effect sizes and different ways to calculate and interpret them. Two important families of effect size in education include those related to:

Correlation
We use correlation when we have matched numerical data (for example, the height and weight of a group of individuals). We can use this type of data to estimate the strength of the relationship between the two variables and explain how much variation within one can be predicted by the other (for example, how much variation in weight can be predicted or explained by variation in height).

Differences
We focus on differences when quantitative data is available for two groups, and we want to estimate the magnitude of the difference between them. For example, this might be pre- or post-test data for a group of students or could be test data for an experimental group and control group. Cohen's d, or standardized mean difference, is one of more common ways to quantify effect size related to difference. Cohen's d is defined as the difference between two means divided by a standard deviation for the data.

Within these two families, there are many different flavours of effect size to choose from depending on the exact specifics of the data to be analysed. And while they cannot all be directly equated, some can be converted to allow for comparison. For example, converting between correlation coefficient and Cohen's d (and vice versa) is relatively simple using the appropriate formula.

An important consideration when considering effect sizes is that the data from which they are calculated can be collected in many different ways. For instance, when considering differences, an important question is, are we looking at the difference between two groups (i.e., a control group versus an experimental group) or the same group over time (i.e., pre- vs post-test)? The answer to this can have important implications for interpreting and making meaning of the effect sizes reported.

Beyond the effect sizes that emerge from individual studies, we also have effect sizes calculated using the statistical process known as meta-analysis. Meta-analysis is a methodology used to summarise the results of several studies addressing the same question. Some of the most publicised researchers use effect sizes (see the work of John Hattie and Robert Marzano), as have many research bodies in education (see the Education Endowment Fund and What Works Clearinghouse).

Effect sizes and meta-analyses are not without their critics, they do have limitations, and they have been controversial in at least some circles. It is beyond the remit of this book to address these concerns in-depth, but I will leave you with Coe's (2018) statement regarding effect size, which I agree with entirely:

> *To adapt Churchill's famous quotation about democracy, systematic review based on effect sizes is probably the worst possible way to summarise what we know about the impact of interventions, apart from all the other ways that have been tried ... it isn't perfect; we do need to understand the limitations; ideally, we need better studies and better reviews.*

Please note, in this book, I refer to effect sizes related to interventions or strategies. Sometimes I do this with the abbreviation ES. Unless there is a direct citation wherever this occurs, I am drawing upon Professor John Hattie's ongoing *Visible Learning* research and using the most up-to-date values that are available online via: <https://www.visiblelearningmetax.com/>.

CHAPTER 1

It's the Vibe

LEARNING INTENTIONS

This chapter focuses on several related features of the classroom. Firstly, we consider the importance of teachers and also what works in the classroom. Next, we discuss the nature of students' experiences in the classroom and the types of things that impact their experiences. And, finally, classroom culture, what I call classroom vibe, is proposed as an overarching strategy by which to improve teaching practice and student learning.
   By the conclusion of this chapter, you will have:
- Thought about how our students experience our classrooms and that how they perceive us as teachers can vary considerably.
- Taken time to appreciate that classroom vibe should be the central consideration for improving teacher practice.

THE IMPORTANCE OF TEACHERS

We know from researchers like John Hattie that teachers account for 30% of the variance we see in student achievement (see Figure 1, adapted from Hattie, 2003).
   What Figure 1 shows us is that teachers and what they do matter. As can be seen, teachers are the second largest factor besides the students themselves and the largest within-school lever that we have at our disposal to improve student learning — teachers account for approximately 75% of the within school variation.

Figure 1. What are the Sources of Variation on Student Achievement?

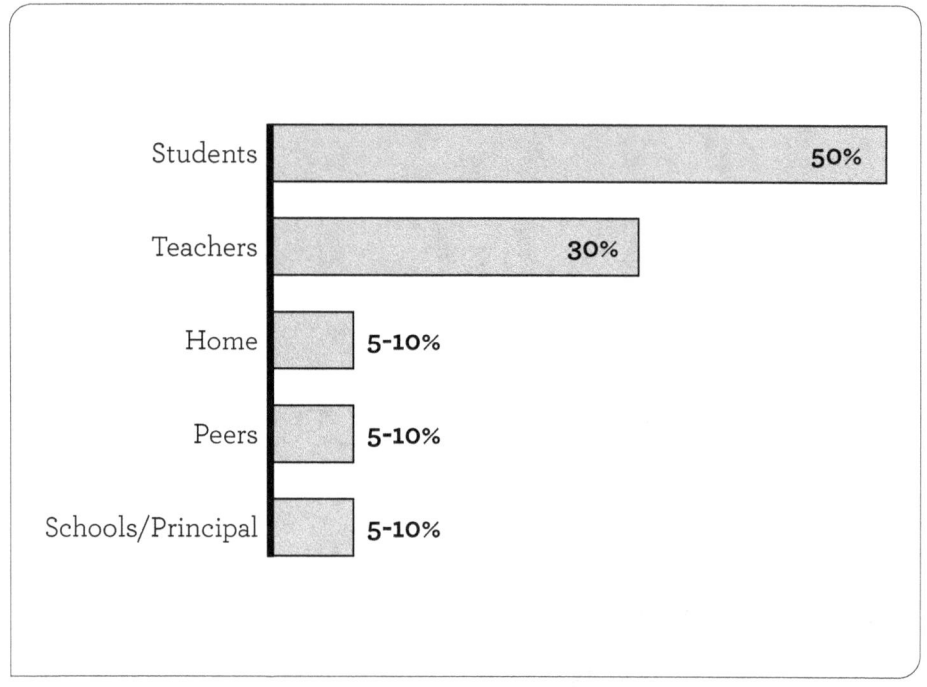

WE KNOW WHAT WORKS

Beyond simply knowing that teachers are important, we also know what teachers should be doing to enhance student learning. Thanks to Hattie (2003, 2008), Marzano (2007) and Rosenshine (2012), there are some excellent comprehensive summaries of the many strategies that our teachers can draw upon that we know impact upon student learning (see Table 1 for some examples).

Given that we know what works, the solution should be relatively simple, right? We know teachers have the biggest influence within the school; we also know what strategies they should be using. Let's get to it!

The issue is that when looking to implement strategies to create change, we ignore something important. It is relatively easy to choose a strategy to implement (although it is not always easy to choose the right or most appropriate strategy). I have seen school leaders make very rash decisions about programs and strategies quite quickly. The real challenge is that implementing most strategies requires much more than 'buying' a program with a manual or simply attending a professional learning session that provides the recipe or steps to follow. The fact is that, as discussed previously, implementation typically requires changes in the values, beliefs, and practices of teachers (and leaders) and can require participants having to learn how to work in new collaborative ways. These changes can be difficult for teachers as they

Table 1. Examples of High Impact Teaching Strategies

Strategy	Effect Size	Description
Cognitive Task Analysis	1.29	Techniques for studying and describing reasoning and knowledge.
Jigsaw Method	1.20	A collaborative learning strategy.
Classroom Discussion	0.82	Instructional strategy by which students are invited to speak with each other about a topic via the use of open questions.
Feedback	0.64	A deliberate strategy by which information is provided that supports learners to decrease the gap between what is known and what is expected to be known.
Questioning	0.48	Educational practice dating back to Greek antiquity through which an agent (i.e., teacher, peer, or textbook) asks factual and conceptual questions.

Note: Adapted from the Visible Learning MetaX (http://www.visiblelearningmetax.com/)

necessitate self-reflection and a capacity to look beyond how they are used to working.

This difference in what is required for change or improvement to occur is essentially the distinction between what Heifetz and Laurie (1997) and Heifetz and Linksy (2002) and have called technical versus adaptive challenges. Specifically, technical challenges are those in which the problem of practice is relatively easy to identify and can be solved using existing knowledge or strategies. In contrast, adaptive challenges are those in which the problem is difficult to identify, and the solution often requires new knowledge and necessitates changes to personal values and beliefs. This distinction is critical to consider as Heifetz has indicated that one of the great improvement failures is misdiagnosing adaptive challenges as technical challenges and seeking out inappropriate solutions.

An excellent example to highlight the differences in change required is, again, differentiation. Often when we think of differentiation, we think of grouping students. Unfortunately, the result is typically using the same approaches to teaching with more homogenous groups of students. It is more powerful to think about differentiation as an amalgam of strategies to be drawn upon to maximize the learning of all students. For example, differentiation might involve teachers not labelling students and maintaining high expectations for all students; formative evaluation of teaching and learning; classroom discussion; effective questioning; and learning intentions with success criteria, all with the goal of being responsive to our students' needs. The distinction here is seeing differentiation as a grouping process over a need to develop flexibility in one's teaching practice. The actual implementation challenge is then changing teachers' beliefs about their role in teaching and how differentiation fits relative to these beliefs.

Related to this, no matter how good a strategy is, no matter how good the supporting research, it is unlikely to succeed without the necessary cultural ingredients or readiness as the first step. Supporting this is the quote from Peter Drucker: "culture eats strategy for breakfast." This implies that a company's success depends on the culture first and strategy second – it's all about the vibe.

The importance of culture is not just relevant to business, though. It is equally crucial in education. For example, you have undoubtedly experienced elements of school culture, team culture, or classrooms that have been counterproductive. For instance, passive-aggressive behaviour, poor communication, lack of transparency, and collaboration are symptoms of a culture that inhibits effective work and implementation of strategy. Within the context of education, MacNeil and colleagues' (2009) work has highlighted the importance of school culture and healthy learning environments on student achievement. Further, the work of Leithwood and his colleagues has shown that the true impact of leadership is first and foremost a result of the culture created (for an excellent summary, see Leithwood et al., 2019). Hattie's meta-synthesis also highlights the importance of classroom climate and cohesion and their potential to impact student learning.

The implication is that within education, within our schools, within our classrooms, focusing on culture is a critical strategy whether you are a teacher or a school leader.

HOW STUDENTS EXPERIENCE THEIR TEACHERS

Despite evidence presented in the introduction that the underlying motivations attracting people into the teaching profession are generally positive, this does not mean all teachers are equal.

To test this, let us engage in a thought experiment. Close your eyes and take a few moments to remember your time at school:

Can you remember any of your teachers?

If so, how did they impact you and your learning?

How have they impacted your life since leaving school?

I have asked many people to think about these questions and they find it easy to recall snippets of their memories, experiences, and emotions from their time at school. But, when pressed to talk about the teachers, I find that two broad categories surface time and time again. I call them the *Famous* and the *Infamous*.

Firstly, the *Famous*. Very often, people readily remember those teachers that cared for them, and who were supportive and passionate. These are the teachers whose passion is often imprinted quietly, deep within us. They turn us onto their passions and help shape our lives.

Secondly *Infamous*. The second category of teachers that crops up is those who remain in our memory because they were unforgettably dull and boring or, worse still, intimidating and demeaning. These teachers also shaped our lives, but not necessarily in a positive sense. In reality, they may have turned us off their subjects. In my role as a secondary school mathematics teacher, I would occasionally come across students who had switched off from learning mathematics as they felt incapable of understanding the subject. Careful probing would usually bring to the surface a negative experience with one of these infamous teachers who had tarnished their experience of the subject.

In addition to these two categories, there is an implied third category. Those teachers that we simply do not remember, those I call the *Forgettables*. These are the teachers who are a blur or blank in our minds. They might have taught, tested, and even entertained us but somehow were too vanilla to have left a mark.

The takeaway here is that as teachers, we leave an impression on our students' experiences of school and the classroom and how it makes them feel. These feelings, whether positive, negative, or ambivalent, will endure over time.

My question to you is:

Which type of teacher do you want to be?

SO, WHAT MAKES THE DIFFERENCE IN STUDENT EXPERIENCE?

What is it about these different groups of teachers that creates such a diverse range of experiences for students?

I do not doubt that there are many contributing factors. We already know that many things that teachers CAN make a difference. My essential argument is that the most critical factor in this variation of memory is not what we as teachers teach but rather the culture or vibe of the classrooms within which we teach. Indeed, Hattie's synthesised literature has indicated that in classrooms with cohesion, with teachers and students who work together and learning spaces perceived as both fair and respectful and focused on supporting all students, the impact on student learning is above average.

While a classroom's culture or vibe is of critical importance, there is clear evidence that there is significant variation in how students perceive this vibe. Having had the opportunity and privilege to analyse student perceptions of teaching practice data collected across tens of thousands of students, thousands of teachers, and hundreds of schools, I feel pretty comfortable in saying that the variation seen is quite stark.

To illustrate the extent of variation, let's consider some data collected with a survey that I have created, the *Classroom Vibe Student Perception of Teaching Survey*. This survey, like this book, has been a labour of love for me. I have used these types of surveys for my whole career. However, this one was created over the last three years drawing upon the ideas underpinning this book combined with my Ph.D. research focused on reporting educational data. The survey was co-designed iteratively, with feedback from teachers and students to support clear communication from students to teachers about how they experience the teaching and learning in a classroom. The purpose of this was to support teacher reflection upon classroom practice with the goal of improvement. This purpose is 100% aligned with the key intention of this book. If you would like to know a bit more about the *Classroom Vibe Student Perceptions of Teaching Survey*, have a look at the website <classroomvibe.com.au>.

As a brief background, my survey was designed to collect and report evidence about eight domains of classroom practice. These domains are related to Teacher Credibility and Teacher Clarity, two high-impact strategies related to how students perceive a teacher's capacity to impact their learning. We will learn more about these two influences later.

While each of the domains of practice captured across teacher credibility and teacher clarity are important, a standout for me when thinking about the climate or culture of the classroom is the nature and status of Trusting Relationships in the classroom. This is because trust is fundamental to all relationships, including the teacher-student relationships. The Trusting Relationship domain of the *Classroom Vibe Student Perception of Teaching Survey* is comprised of five statements related to observable teacher behaviours and actions that are known to build trust. The survey asks students to indicate the frequency with which their teacher displays each behavior on a five-point scale.

Example statements include:
- My teacher treats students fairly; and
- My teacher encourages respectful behaviour in our classroom.

Figure 2 visualizes the range in mean rating of teachers amongst all classrooms that have to date completed the survey. What should be clear is that the variation which exists is considerable.

Figure 2. How Do Student Perceptions about Trusting Relationships Vary?

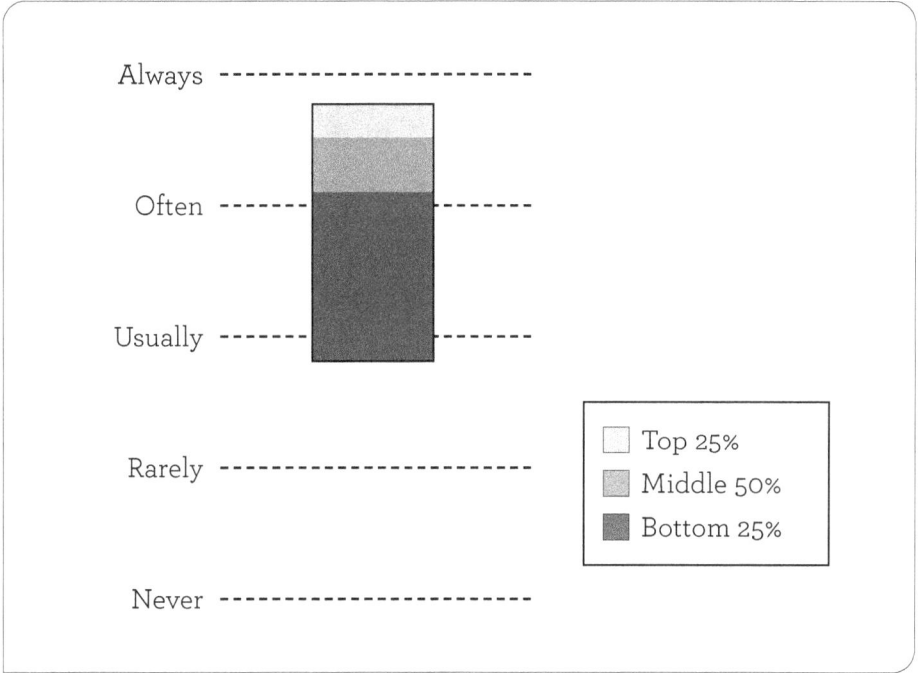

This variation is perhaps more meaningfully illustrated in Figure 3, which highlights the mean rating of four individual classes. As is evident, there are discernible differences in how students perceived the nature of trusting relationships between each of these classes. In particular, on average, the students in Class 2 perceived the level of Trusting Relationships to be considerably lower than the other three classes. The fact that such differences exist is probably not a surprise, given our reflections on teachers earlier. But what might be a surprise is that these four classes were all taught by the same teacher during the same semester.

Figure 4 provides a different lens for considering the data for each of the four classes displayed in Figure 2, highlighting the variation of student perceptions *within* each class.

Figure 3. Student Perceptions of Teaching of Four Example Classes

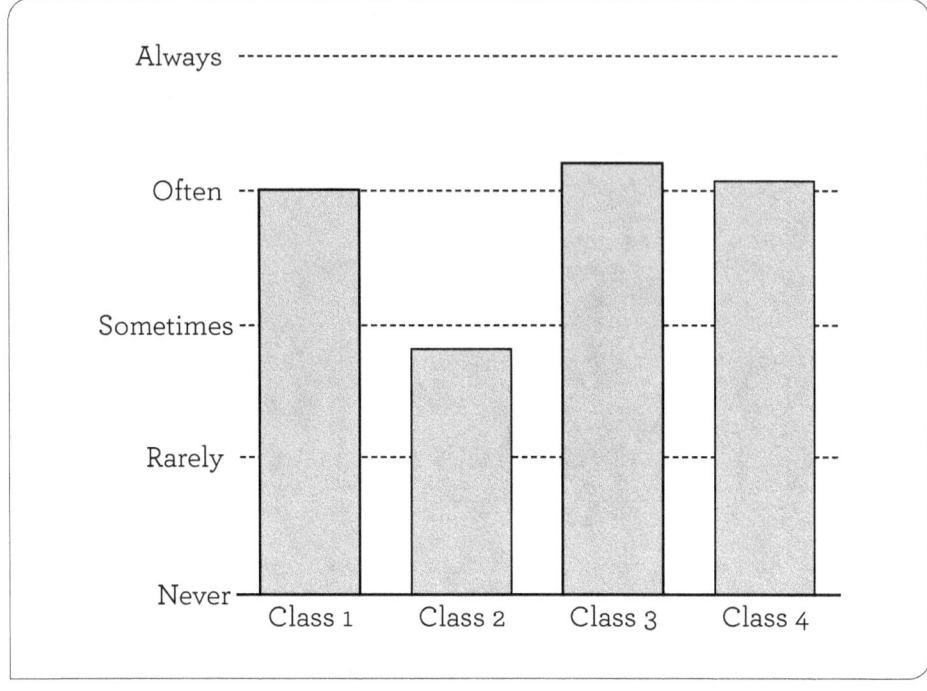

Figure 4. Variation in Student Perceptions Within and Between Classes

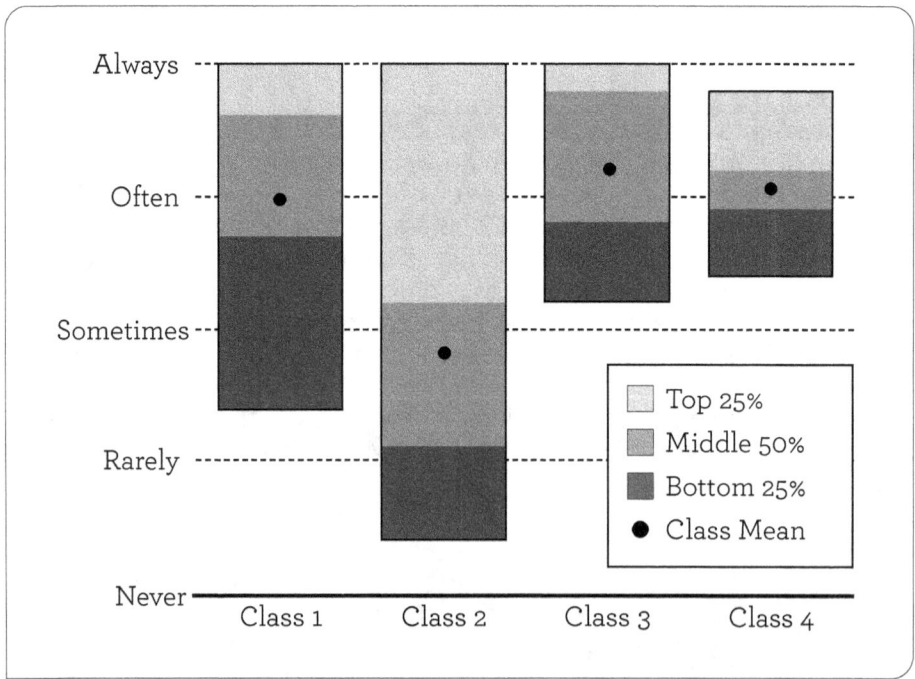

What should now be evident is that while there is a clear difference *between* classes, there is also considerable variation in how the teacher is perceived *within* each class. For example, consider Class 2. The mean rating is the lowest of the four classes but with considerable variation within the class. Indeed, some students feel positive about their experiences within this classroom, and others have almost the opposite experience. Or perhaps consider Class 1 and Class 4. While the mean rating for each class is similar, there is much more variation in Class 1 than in Class 4.

Several questions provoke my curiosity at this point.
- How can students experience their teacher so differently?
- How can different classes experience the same teacher so differently?
- How can students within a single class experience the same teacher so differently?

To answer these questions is not simple. However, I argue that the variation we see is the consequence of what we do as teachers. That is, how we behave in class, carrying ourselves with humility and confidence, listening to and talking with our students, looking at them, smiling and laughing with them, moving around the classroom with ease to support them as we share our knowledge and lives with them. The differences in how we behave across each of these things is what has the impact. This is about how our behaviours cultivate the learning-focused atmosphere in our classrooms, what I call a classroom's vibe, and how the students experience it.

The implication of all this is clear. As I see it, there is a compelling opportunity to enhance students' perceptions of the culture or vibe within our classrooms. This enhancement is much more than improving average ratings on a questionnaire about our students' perceptions of a classroom's vibe. Yes, as we will see later, these ratings are important, but it is also about seeking to minimize the range of student experience that we see both within and between classrooms. The thing is, I firmly believe that as teachers, it is our responsibility to seek to understand the variation in student experience that exists within our classes and simultaneously aim to lift the average while minimising the variation.

Further, I believe that it is the responsibility of school leaders to create structures and processes to support teachers to focus on this kind of improvement. For me, this is a matter of equity. All students deserve to have positive experiences in our classrooms. As the adults in the room, I contend that teachers have the moral imperative to take ownership of this through the intentional relationships we nurture with ALL our students and facilitate between our students. Only by stepping up to this challenge can we enhance our classroom vibe, student engagement, and ultimately learning.

> *In summing up it's the atmosphere,
> it's the culture, it's the climate,
> it's the community, it's the connections,
> it's the vibe and, no that's it, it's the vibe. I rest my case.*[3]

IT'S THE VIBE

When I look back on my own experiences as a beginning teacher, I do not doubt that I made mistakes in how I cultivated my classrooms. The effects still resonate with me now. Despite having the best interests of my students at heart, I created unnecessary frustration and conflict for both my students and me. With hindsight, I see that the atmosphere I nurtured was wrong. It was not learning-focused. It was teaching-focused. My students perceived this, and my classroom culture, the vibe, suffered.

For me now, this notion of classroom vibe is fundamental in our schools. I wish I had considered it much earlier in my career.

So, how might we take this nebulous idea and define classroom culture in a simple, actionable framework?

To help answer this question, Table 2 summarises a selection of known high-impact influences that contribute to the learning-focused atmosphere of the classroom experienced by the students, what I call classroom vibe. Looking at all these influences, it can seem unclear where to start, particularly as we have already established that many strategies can or might work. Based on my experiences as a teacher and leader and reading the contemporary literature, I propose two vital influences that allow us to focus on building classroom vibe. These are firstly, Teacher Credibility which is about the perceived trustworthiness of a teacher through the eyes of their students. And secondly, Teacher Clarity, which is about students' perceptions of the capacity of a teacher to convey to their students a complete understanding about what their students are to learn. For me, Teacher Credibility and Teacher Clarity are standout influences for two reasons. First, because they both have relatively high effect sizes. And, second, because they are umbrella influences that incorporate, or cover, many other known high-impact strategies, including most of the other factors listed in Table 2; this is illustrated in Table 3. For these two reasons, Teacher Credibility and Teacher Clarity represent a great place to start.

Table 2. High Impact Teaching Strategies Related to Classroom Climate

Strategy	Effect Size	Description
Belonging	0.40	The degree to which students feel as though they are included, accepted, encouraged, and respected by others.
Feedback	0.64	A deliberate strategy by which information is provided to support a learner to decrease the disparity between what they know and what they are expected to know.
Humour	0.04	The use of humour to build a safe learning environment and nurture teacher-student relations.
Immediacy	0.66	Teacher behaviours that communicate approachability.
Praise	0.12	Expressing approval or admiration of a student or their performances.
Teacher Clarity	0.76	Student perceptions regarding the quality of their teacher's organization, explanation, examples and guided practice, and assessment of student learning.
Teacher Credibility	1.09	Student perceptions regarding the quality of their teacher's competence, trustworthiness, and perceived caring.
Teacher Expectations	0.43	The expectations about student performance held by teachers.
Teacher Personality	0.24	Personality factors including the big five personality traits (i.e., such as openness to experience, conscientiousness, extraversion, agreeableness, and neuroticism).
Teacher Subject Matter Knowledge	0.23	A teacher's pedagogical content knowledge. That is their combined understanding of what to teach and how to teach it.
Teacher Verbal Ability	0.22	The capacity to speak well with high levels of verbal proficiency.
Teacher-Student Relationships	0.48	The quality of the relationship between the teacher and student.

Note: Adapted from the Visible Learning MetaX (http://www.visiblelearningmetax.com/)

Table 3. High Impact Influences Within Teacher Credibility and Teacher Clarity.

Teacher Credibility (ES: 1.09)	Teacher Clarity (ES: 0.76)
The term is used to describe whether a teacher is considered (by their students) to be *"believable, convincing, and capable of persuading students that they can be successful."* (Fisher & Frey, 2018).	Teacher Clarity is *"a measure of the clarity of communication between teachers and students."* (Fendick, 1990, p. 10)
Trusting Relationships	Organisation
Competence	Explanation
Passion	Examples and Guided Practice
Immediacy	Assessment of Learning

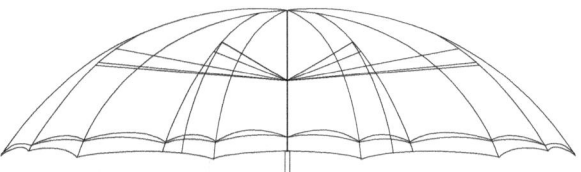

Related Influences
Strong Classroom Cohesion (0.53)
Teacher-Student Relationships (0.48)
Teacher Expectations (0.43)
Belonging (0.4)
Classroom Management (0.35)
Decreasing Disruptive Behaviour (0.34)
Teacher Personality (0.24)
Teacher Subject Matter Knowledge (0.23)
Teacher Verbal Ability (0.22)
Humour (0.04)
Students Feeling Disliked (-0.13)

Related Influences
Testing (1.07)
Success Criteria (0.88)
Micro-Teaching (0.88)
Classroom Discussion (0.82)
Appropriately Challenging Goals (0.59)
Feedback (0.64)
Mastery Learning (0.61)
Direct Instruction (0.59)
Scaffolding and Situated Learning (0.58)
Explicit Teaching Strategies (0.57)
Clear Goal Intentions (0.51)
Questioning (0.48)
Student Rating of Teacher Quality (0.43)
Behaviour/Advance Organisers (0.42)
Worked Examples (0.37)
Formative Evaluation (034)
Frequent Testing (0.33)
Praise (0.12)

Note: Adapted from the Visible Learning MetaX (http://www.visiblelearningmetax.com/)

A reminder that when thinking about enhancing the vibe in the classroom, what is experienced by our students is what matters, and how we make them feel in our classrooms. It is not how we as teachers feel, or if we think that the vibe is okay.

Unpacking Teacher Credibility

Teacher Credibility is about a teacher's trustworthiness or believability and is a necessary ingredient for classroom vibe. According to Fisher and Frey (2018), teacher credibility is about whether a teacher is, in the eyes of their students, "believable, convincing, and capable of persuading students that they can be successful." Teacher credibility is more than just about trust or belief in a broad sense but in the sense that a teacher can positively impact student learning.

The research tells us that Teacher Credibility is a vital influence in ensuring student learning. In fact, with an effect size of 1.09, there is clear evidence that if students see their teachers as credible, they believe that they are more likely to succeed and subsequently do. Indeed, as Hattie has indicated, if you ask a student before they walk into their class whether this teacher is credible or will have an impact on your learning, and they say no, the day is over.

But what does it mean for a teacher to be credible?

What is the basis for this belief and trust?

As we have identified, Teacher Credibility is not simply a matter of students 'liking' their teacher. It is about whether they perceive them as being a teacher who will enhance their learning, about how a teacher's behaviours cultivate this and contribute to the vibe of the classroom. The history of Teacher Credibility research dates back over half a decade. Over this time, the conception of Teacher Credibility has evolved to include four key elements. These include a teacher's:

1. Perceived capacity to build trusting, productive relationships;
2. Competence as a leader of learning;
3. Passion and dynamism in the classroom; and
4. Presence and availability or immediacy to support student learning (see Haskin, 2000).

Further, I have added a fifth element, impact, which focuses on a teacher's capacity to influence student learning positively.

Chapter 3 will provide a brief description of each of these and, more importantly, include strategies for enhancing each to support teachers to improve their classroom practice.

Unpacking Teacher Clarity

Teacher Clarity is conceptualized as the measure of transparency in communication between a teacher and their students (Fendick, 1990). Teacher Clarity is vital to ensuring students learn. In fact, with an effect size of 0.76, there is strong evidence that students taught by a teacher with a high degree of clarity in their communication are more likely to succeed.

Teacher Clarity is more than whether a teacher speaks clearly and is easily understood (i.e., they do not mumble); this bar is way too low. Indeed, for a teacher to truly demonstrate Teacher Clarity means that they have complete confidence in and understanding of what their students are to learn in an upcoming unit of work *before* planning instruction and assessment, AND they can convey this confidence to their students. Teacher Clarity is then not one but many aspects of teaching captured across the four areas introduced by Fendick (1990). These include clarity through demonstrated ability to:
1. Organise student learning coherently;
2. Introduce new learning;
3. Support new learning with examples and guided practice; and
4. Capacity to embed a variety of assessment practice effectively into practice.

Chapter 4 will focus on unpacking these four factors and outline strategies to support teachers in improving their classroom practice accordingly.

MAKING YOUR VIBE YOUR STRATEGY

Seeing classroom culture or vibe through the lens of high-impact strategies as proposed allows us to see vibe as the strategy. Indeed, realizing a classroom's culture through the dual lens of the two influences, Teacher Credibility and Teacher Clarity, provides a simple yet powerful framework that allows teachers to focus on targeting culture as their improvement strategy in a way that integrates many high yield strategies. My essential argument is that if you want to improve student learning, it's all about the vibe.

Taking an approach that integrates the high-impact strategies embedded in Teacher Credibility and Teacher Clarity to build culture is key to building a vibrant classroom room of engaged learners (see Figure 5). This vibrancy is what I like to call a Classroom's Vibe, the learning-focused atmosphere of a classroom experienced by the students.

Fundamentally, a vibrant classroom, a class with vibe, does not just happen. It is the deliberate, intentional consequence of the relationships that educators cultivate, through their behaviour, with their students along with the competence and passion they demonstrate for their practice. The underlying theory of change is that by focusing upon enhancing the inter-related concepts of Teacher Credibility and Teacher Clarity, a teacher will improve their students' experiences of a Classroom's Vibe. In the first instance, the result is enhanced student

Figure 5. Teacher Credibility + Teacher Clarity = A Classroom with Vibe

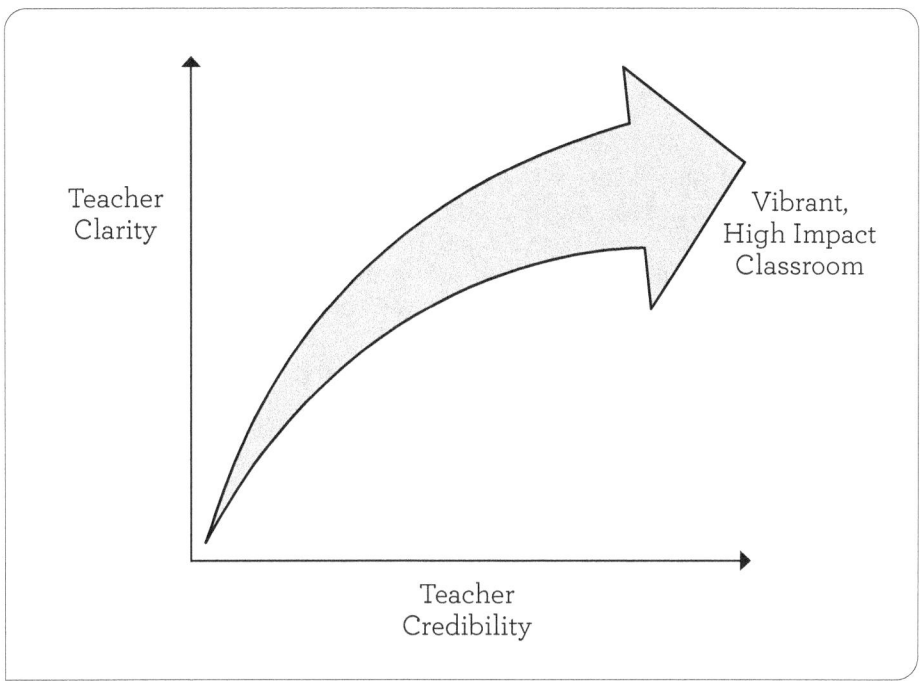

Figure 6. The Classroom Vibe Theory of Change

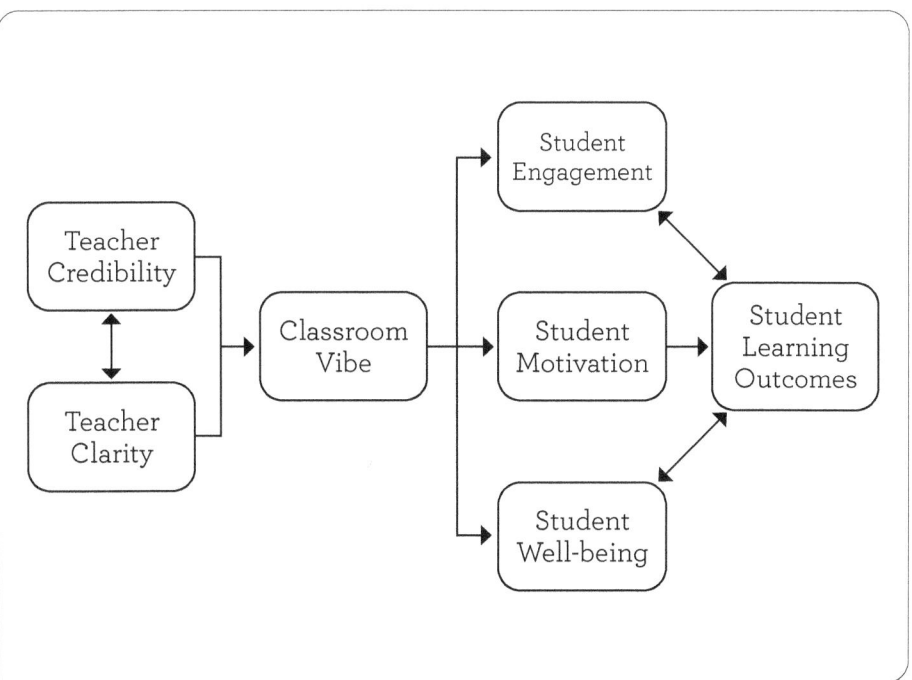

engagement in learning, motivation, and well-being. Ultimately, the result is improved student learning outcomes. This is better captured in Figure 6.

CHAPTER SUMMARY – WHY IS THIS IMPORTANT?

This chapter has raised several key points to consider:
- We remember those teachers who had a positive impact on us.
- Classroom cohesion or climate can have an above-average impact on student learning. It is worth paying attention to developing classes as inviting places for students to come and learn.
- Despite the intentions our teachers bring, our students' experiences of teachers can vary widely both within and between classes.
- The variation we see between classes and teachers is linked to the climate and culture our students experience in the classroom.

REFLECTION QUESTIONS

Take some time to reflect on and answer each of these questions. Make notes or draw pictures.
    Do whatever helps you process the ideas and concepts discussed, and if you feel comfortable, share your answers with a colleague.

- Why did you become a teacher?

- What are some of the classroom experiences you remember from your time at school?

- Who was your best teacher, and why? Who was your worst teacher, and why?

- How would you like your students to remember their experiences in your class?

- What are you doing in your practice to ensure this happens?

- How do you know what you are doing is working?

- When you think about some of the strategies you have implemented over the years, how successful have you been?

- What types of things have helped you to be successful in trialling new ideas?

- What types of things have impacted your ability?

- How would you describe the vibe in your classrooms? How would you know?

- What sort of things do you do to enhance your classroom vibe?

CHAPTER 2

Nurturing Classroom Vibe

LEARNING INTENTIONS

This chapter introduces the Classroom Vibe Inquiry Cycle, a comprehensive process to engage in reflection about teaching practice that will yield evidence about a teacher's current practice that can be used to drive improvements efforts now and into the future.

By the conclusion of this chapter, you will have:
- Some practical strategies to collect evidence regarding classroom vibe
- A process to support active inquiry into tour classroom vibe.

Please note, this chapter includes several template examples. A blank copy of each is included in the appendices for your reference.

So far, this book has presented what I consider a compelling case regarding the importance of improving classroom climate or what I call a classroom's vibe. As a reminder, I propose that a classroom's vibe, the learning-focused atmosphere of the classroom experienced by the students, is the consequence of building a teacher's credibility and clarity. Teacher Credibility and Teacher Clarity are, in turn, the result of focusing improvement efforts on behaviours that enhance student sentiment about a teacher's credibility and clarity.

Teacher Credibility is built by enhancing the:
- Capacity to building trusting, productive relationships.
- Competence as a leader of learning.
- Passion in the classroom.
- Presence and availability to support student learning.
- Capacity to impact upon student learning.

Teacher Clarity is built by enhancing the:
- Ability to organise student learning coherently.
- Capacity to introduce new learning.
- Support of new learning with examples and guided practice.
- Capacity to embed assessment effectively into practice.

There will be more about how to build these in Chapters 3 and 4.

My position is that without drawing upon a structured approach to integrate new skills and strategies into practice then things are unlikely to change. Now is perhaps a good time to pause and remember the cognitive biases that we mentioned earlier and think about how that might interfere with our capacity to improve (see pages 6–8).

CLASSROOM VIBE INQUIRY CYCLE

To support teachers in thinking about how they might build their classroom vibe, I present a cycle of reflection that a teacher can use either by themselves or with peers to inquire into their practice through the lens of Classroom Vibe and make improvements. I want to briefly point out that this cycle of inquiry is not dissimilar to many of the other inquiry cycles you may have seen previously, so it should not be seen as something 'new' or foreign.

Figure 7. Classroom Vibe Inquiry Cycle.

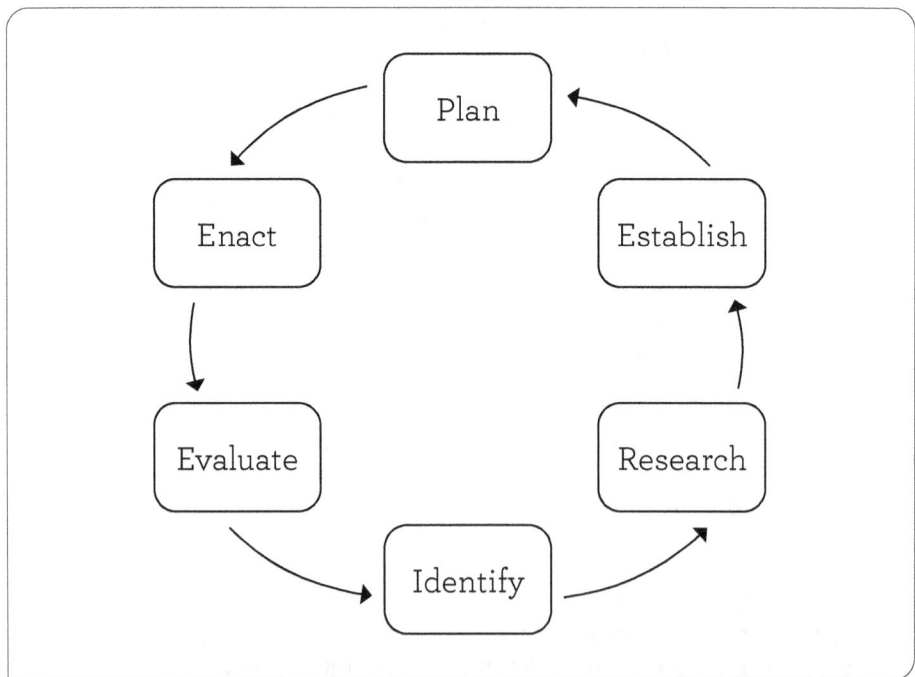

There are six steps in the Classroom Vibe Inquiry Cycle focused on supporting teachers to understand and improve their practice. Each of these steps will be outlined over the following pages.

Step 1. Identify (Practice-Based Need)

I believe that decisions about improvement efforts, whether for a teacher or school, need to be based on fact, not fancy. When I say fancy, I mean that improvement efforts should not focus on what someone is interested in working on, what their interest might be, or what they heard someone say at a conference. Instead, what they work on should be grounded in evidence.

Why, might you ask? Shouldn't teachers have agency over their professional learning?

My response would be an enthusiastic yes! Of course, teachers should have some agency over their professional learning, but it needs to be within reason. I would argue that this agency should be exercised over process and product, not the focus area of their professional learning. It should also be agency to pursue a common goal as opposed to a personal area of interest.

Again, why, you might ask?

Well, the reason relates to the cognitive biases we discussed earlier in the book. Let me remind you.

Firstly, the illusory superiority bias, which is is the cognitive bias by which we are not a very good judge of our ability. This bias means that we do not always have a good sense of our strengths (and weaknesses). The implication here is that what we think we need to focus on improving is possibly not what we actually need to improve. As such, if left to our own devices, we may potentially waste time focusing our efforts on the wrong things.

Secondly, if you remember, confirmation bias shows that we seek out things that quite literally confirm our beliefs. The implication is that we may seek out opportunities for improvement that likely align with our existing beliefs and practices. As such, if left to our own devices, we may potentially focus on things we already know and are doing.

So, where does this leave us?

It leaves us needing to find objective evidence about our practice to discover what we need to improve. I contend that it is only through drawing upon evidence about our practice that we can accurately IDENTIFY opportunities for improvement. Indeed, if you think back to Chapter 1, the collection of evidence to support is critical. Remember that the TNTP (2015) lamented that while teachers needed information about their strengths and weaknesses to help them improve their instruction, they weren't getting it. Further, collecting evidence also has the added benefit of creating baseline data against which we can compare data collected in the future to help us make inferences about our improvement efforts.

Now, then, is an excellent opportunity to drop a quote I like to use, which draws upon the words of two great Americans: Bill Bullard, School Leader, and W. Edwards Deming, engineer, statistician, and management expert.

Without data, you are just another person with an opinion, and opinion is the lowest form of human knowledge requiring no understanding or accountability.

So how might we go about collecting objective evidence of our practice?

I have to say I am glad you asked, as this is a topic I love talking about.

In reality, many strategies can be used to gain insights into the effectiveness and impact of teaching. For example, one of the critical messages of Hattie's *Visible Learning* is "Know thy impact." This message directs teachers to appreciate and evaluate the effectiveness of their teaching through seeking 'visible' evidence of student learning via the use of pre- and post-tests or artefacts of learning. While this may be an excellent place to start, it may not necessarily provide nuanced insight into what is and is not working in terms of teacher practice. In which case, we need to consider other potential opportunities such as self-appraisal, micro-teaching, peer observation, and student perceptions of teaching.

Firstly, self-reflection or self-appraisal is a simple yet powerful approach to gain insights into one practice that can help identify opportunities for improvement. Rather than reflecting generally on one's practice, it makes sense to reflect on an objective rubric to avoid being compromised by our cognitive biases. To support such reflection, I have included a simple matrix in Table 4.

Table 4. Classroom Vibe – Self-Assessment Rubric

	Description	Disagree	Kind of Disagree	Kind of Agree	Agree	Strongly Agree
Teacher Credibility						
Trusting Relationships	I try to engage, connect with and support my students regularly and build healthy relationships in the classroom.					
Competence	I prepare for my classes in advance, have clear expectations for learning, and am confident in the classroom.					
Passion	I enjoy teaching my subject and try to communicate this enthusiasm to my students.					
Presence	I am available to help support my students in their learning.					
Impact	I understand the impact I have on my students learning and help my students see their growth.					
Teacher Clarity						
Organisation	I map out and clarify the purpose of learning and how it links to past and future learning for my students. I create opportunities for reviewing what has been learned and make work appropriately challenging for all students.					
Explanation	I make sure that my students understand the language and knowledge of what is being taught, and I respond to their needs as I teach.					
Examples & Guided Practice	I use worked examples regularly throughout my teaching and incorporate opportunities for my students to practice into my lessons.					
Assessment	I make clear the purpose of assessment to my students and use assessment practice holistically as a part of my teaching.					

Next, micro-teaching is an approach to teacher professional learning where a teacher videos a class and then reviews it back to gain constructive feedback. This method was created by Professor Dwight W. Allen from Stanford University. With an effect size of 0.88, micro-teaching is a powerful, high-impact strategy for improving teacher practice. I have included a simple matrix in Table 5 to support help you review your class through the dual lenses of Classroom Vibe.

Peer observation is very similar to micro-teaching. The critical difference is that observations are made by a peer or colleague as opposed to the teacher. Peer observation can happen live, or you can video a class and share it with a colleague (or team of colleagues) to review and provide feedback. The matrix in Table 5 can be used for peer-reviewing a class.

A further suggestion concerning micro-teaching and peer observation is the possibility of combining the two strategies so that each teacher in a team takes a turn to record a class and then shares the video with the group to gain feedback. Such an approach introduces the powerful possibility for teachers to discuss and moderate their understanding of high-impact strategies and what they look like in the classroom.

And, finally, Student Perceptions of Teacher Practice. Drawing on students' perceptions of teaching is one of my favorite approaches for making evidence about teaching visible. Indeed, I have used various strategies since the start of my career. There are several reasons why I like student perception surveys. Firstly, with an overall effect size of 0.45, the evidence base shows that student ratings of the quality of teaching is a potentially high-impact strategy. Further, research has shown that compared to other strategies (i.e., classroom observation), student perceptions of teaching collected using student surveys are more reliable in predicting impact upon learning (Balch, 2012; Kane & Cantrell, 2010). Research has also shown that students, and their perceptions of teacher practice, are trustworthy sources of insight into the quality of teaching, which can be a powerful source of ideas for how a teacher practice might be improved (MET Project, 2012).

There are many student perception surveys available to collect evidence from students. Table 6 provides a brief set of survey questions to act as a starting point. If you want to learn about the survey I have designed, look at Classroom Vibe (classroomvibe.com.au).

Table 5. Micro-Teaching & Observation Assessment Rubric

	Description	Disagree	Kind of Disagree	Kind of Agree	Agree	Strongly Agree
Teacher Credibility						
Trusting Relationships	The teacher engaged positively with students and made opportunities for students to interact in meaningful ways that built culture in the classroom.					
Competence	The teacher engaged in a way that communicated competence, including being confident, comfortable, and in control of the classroom.					
Passion	The teacher's passion for their subject and teaching was evident.					
Presence	The teacher was available to support the learning of their students. They were expressive, making eye contact, using students' names and inclusive language, and moving around the room to students when needed.					
Teacher Clarity						
Organisation	The teacher made the purpose of learning explicit to students. The work was appropriately challenging for all students. The teacher took time to support their students review what has been learned.					
Explanation	The teacher tried to build student knowledge in an engaging manner. They used formative techniques while teaching to ensure students understood what is being taught, and responded was necessary.					
Examples & Guided Practice	The teacher showed students how to succeed in this class. The model worked examples and provided the opportunity for students to practice their new knowledge and skills.					
Assessment	The teacher clarified how students would be assessed in this class and used formative assessment strategies as part of their teaching.					

Table 6. Sample Student Perception of Teaching Questions

	Example Questions	Disagree	Kind of Disagree	Kind of Agree	Agree	Strongly Agree
Teacher Credibility						
Trusting Relationships	I feel trusted by my teacher. I feel safe coming to this class.					
Competence	I feel confident that I am learning new things in this class. I know what I am supposed to be doing in this class.					
Passion	My teacher is enthusiastic about this subject. I feel excited about learning in this class.					
Presence	My teacher is available to me learn. My teacher moves around the room to help us.					
Teacher Clarity						
Organisation	My teacher explains the purpose of what we learn. My teacher regularly reviews what we have learned.					
Explanation	My teacher explains new ideas and concepts clearly. My teacher helps me understand the language of this subject.					
Examples & Guided Practice	My teacher shows me what I need to do to succeed. In class, we have the chance to practice what we learn.					
Assessment	I understand how I will be assessed in this class. My teacher checks what we know before moving on.					

While many forms of data are available, I would recommend Student Perceptions of Teaching for this phase. This is because, the way I see it and have defined it, a classroom's vibe is the learning-focused atmosphere of the classroom as *experienced* by the students. As such, it is crucial to gain evidence straight from the source.

Once you have collected evidence using one of the above strategies, it is possible to interrogate the data and determine which aspect of your practice needs attention.

The Power of Student Perceptions

I have worked with many teachers over the years to think about collecting evidence from their students to gain insights that can support reflection and improvement efforts.

When I think about them, one stands out above them all as demonstrative of the power of student perception. And this is a teacher, let's call her here Ms M.

Ms M worked in a large international school in Malaysia, teaching Year 5 students. Our work together began when she ran an earlier version of the Classroom Vibe Student Perception Survey.

Ms M was quite pleased with some of the feedback she received from her students. In particular, there was a strong sense that she encouraged respectful relationships in the classroom, acted confidently, and had clear expectations for behaviour.

A big surprise for her was substantial evidence that students did not feel comfortable asking her for help. Nor did they feel comfortable making mistakes.

She was surprised by this because she ran the survey not long after the class had completed a six-month Growth Mindset program.

Following up from the survey, Ms M set the goal of understanding why her students felt they couldn't ask for help. She ran some student focus groups to talk with students and ultimately made some amendments.

When she re-ran the Classroom Vibe survey later in the year, the results were largely comparably except one statement: I feel comfortable asking my teacher for help. Despite the same sample size (i.e., 20 students), Her students' perceptions for this statement had improved considerably (from an average of 3.5 to 4.3).

Step 2. Research (Best Practice Options)

Once you have determined the aspect of your practice to improve, it is necessary to do some RESEARCH to identify options. Now, of course, this book is a great place to start, but many other resources are available to help you.
 A selection is included below:
- The Education Endowment Fund
 <https://educationendowmentfoundation.org.uk/>
- The What Works Clearinghouse
 <https://ies.ed.gov/ncee/wwc/>
- The Learning Scientists
 <https://www.learningscientists.org/>
- Cult of Pedagogy
 <https://www.cultofpedagogy.com/>
- Edutopia
 <https://www.edutopia.org/>
- Visible Learning MetaX
 <https://www.visiblelearningmetax.com/>
- The Best Evidence Encyclopedia
 <https://bestevidence.org/>
- Local Teach Meets
- Twitter Groups
- LinkedIn Networking
- Facebook
- Local and International Professional Associations
- Research Articles
- Peers.

Step 3. Establish (It is Goal Setting Time)

*All successful people have a goal.
No one can get anywhere unless they know
where they want to go and what they want to do.*[4]

Once you have identified the strategy or strategies you will work on, it is essential to commit and ESTABLISH your goal. There are many frameworks to support goal setting. For example:

OKR
OKR is an acronym that stands for Objectives and Key Results. This framework identifies objectives, which define a broad goal. These are then broken into key results and milestones to help measure progress.

SMART

The SMART framework is one of the most well-known for setting goals. The basis is that effective goals must be Specific, Measurable/Meaningful, Achievable, Relevant, and Time-Bound. It was first put forth as a method by Doran (1981). This approach is elaborated upon in Table 7.

SMARTER

The SMARTER framework is a simple extension of the SMART framework to include Evaluate and Readjust, which can help to emphasize the iterative nature of improvement.

Backward Goals

This process is like the Backwards by Design process of curriculum planning developed by Wiggins and McTighe (1998). Essentially, the process begins with identifying the big, overarching goal. You must then work backward, breaking the goal down into smaller 'supporting' goals, which can be divided further into targets and tasks. The result is an actionable roadmap to achieving your goal.

While there are many options for goal setting, I believe the SMART framework provides a simple process that sits well within the Classroom Vibe Inquiry Cycle.

Table 7. SMART Goals Setting Unpacked

S	Specific	Goals should have a narrow focus
M	Meaningful & Measurable	Goals should be powerful and have an impact. They should also be tangible so you understand if you are improving.
A	Actionable & Achievable	Goals should seek to push you beyond your current level of ability or performance but not so far as to be impossible.
R	Realistic & Relevant	Goals should be appropriate for your context and something that is within your capacity to influence.
T	Time-bound	Goals should have a timeframe. I recommend setting short-term micro-goals when setting goals (with a bigger picture goal or direction in mind) as it allows you to be agile.

(Adapted from Doran, 1981)

Beyond simply setting goals blindly, I recommend drawing upon Professor Andrew Martin and his colleagues' work focused on personal best goals. Martin (2006) proposed a personal best goal as one that is specific, challenging, and competitively self-referenced and necessitates a performance standard that matches or betters one's previous best. Studies from this group have shown that setting personal goals is an effective approach to enhancing outcomes (Martin & Elliot, 2015; Ginns, Martin, Durksen, Burns & Pope, 2018). Now, while the work of this group focused on student learning, the lessons are arguably just as applicable to adults. This notion of setting a personal best goal is central to the Classroom Vibe Inquiry Cycle I advocate in this book.

In addition to setting powerful goals, it is also essential to take steps to increase the likelihood that they are achieved. One powerful research-informed strategy is the WOOP framework to individually identify what they want, why it's important, and how to overcome the obstacles that might get in the way. The framework outlined below is not just a good idea. It has been shown to reduce stress and increase engagement, enable problem-solving, and improve time management (Oettingen, 2014).

Wish
This step is about choosing a goal you would like to accomplish. The driving question is: What are you hoping to achieve?

Outcome
This step is about taking time to describe what the best possible outcome would be if you achieved your goal. The driving questions are: What would it look like if you were successful? And how would you feel?

Obstacles
At this point, you are taking time to identify the personal obstacles or barriers that might prevent you from achieving your goal. The driving question is: What could get in the way between you and your goal?

Plan
Finally, you need to plan to overcome each obstacle you have identified. The driving questions are: How will you overcome each of the potential barriers you have identified?

I have created a template to support your goal setting by integrating the ideas captured across the SMART and WOOP frameworks combined with Personal Best goals (see Table 8).

Table 8. Classroom Vibe Goal Setting Template

Evidence-Informed Need What does the evidence tell you that you need to improve next?
Goal Express your goal as a statement. I am committed to …
Outcome What are the best possible outcomes for achieving your goal?
Obstacles What might get in the way of achieving your goal? Express this as a series of "if … then" statements.
Overcome It is time to plan how you might overcome an obstacle that arises?

Step 4. Plan (For Successful Improvement)

With a goal firmly in mind, now is the time to PLAN and map out changes to practice. This step is about deciding exactly how you will put into practice the options you have identified in Step 2. An excellent process to think about for this phase is that of putting together a theory of action or change. If you recall the figure on page 25, a theory of action or change is a linked set of propositions that form a logical chain of reasoning which explains how change or action occurs. Program Evaluation Professionals would undoubtedly take you through a comprehensive process for creating your theory of change, but I recommend using the following template to support your planning.

Table 9.   Planning for Success Template

Goal/Vision: *Briefly summarise your improvement goal.*		
I am committed to improving my capacity to support students to review what has been taught.		
Current Reality	**Strategies / Actions**	**Planned Impact**
Describe what the evidence is telling you.	Describe things you will start doing and stop doing.	Describe the goal state.
My students' perceptions of my classroom were positive BUT highlighted an opportunity to better support my students in reviewing what is being learned during class.	I am going to structure review time into my classes. I am going to keep track of time. I am going to stop rushing through my classes and teaching. I am going to teach my students how to review a topic effectively.	A classroom where I am consciously taking time to support my students review what is being learned, and my students are optimistic about this.

Step 5. Embed (Improvements in the Classroom)

EMBED is about taking the plunge and beginning to make changes to your practice in the classroom. Critical to this is seeking feedback about how effectively you are making changes – this is represented in Figure 8.

Figure 8. Amplifying Improvement with Feedback

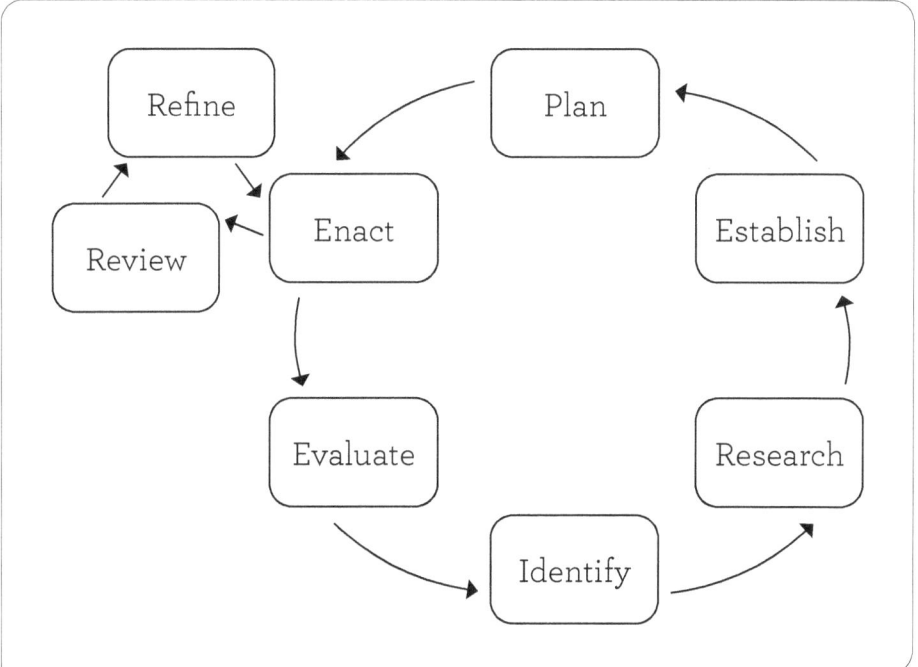

Review
To Review, we seek evidence to understand how improvements are progressing. Like the Identify stage, this evidence may come from various sources, including self-reflection, micro-teaching, peer observation, or student perceptions. I recommend self-reflection, micro-teaching or peer observation.

Refine
To Refine, we respond to feedback and further refine practice to create further improvement.

Re-Enact
To Re-Enact, we are seeking to put into action updated practice.

Note: This cycle of refinement MAY take place several times before progressing onwards.

Step 6. Evaluate (Impact and Improvement)

EVALUATE is the final step in a Classroom Vibe Improvement Cycle. The purpose of this step is to collect evidence after your improvement effort has finished to help you to understand its effectiveness. This will then allow you to celebrate your successes and identify further opportunities for improvement. This stage is not about forming judgment but simply about engaging in authentic reflection upon the efforts you have engaged in to improve your practice.

As in Step 1, the types of evidence you can collect for this stage include self-reflection, micro-teaching, peer observation, and student perceptions of teaching. While there are many forms of data available, I recommend student perceptions of teaching for this step.

IMPROVEMENT IN ACTION

*Practice the philosophy of continuous improvement.
Get a little bit better every single day.*

Brian Tracy, Motivational Speaker & Author

The Classroom Vibe Improvement Cycle should not be seen as something that happens as a once-off. Instead, it must be seen as just one link in an ongoing process of continual improvement over many years and many classes. This is because:
1. There is always an opportunity to improve our practice.
2. Each of our classes experiences us differently.

To support the implementation of ongoing improvement cycles, Table 10 includes a summary of suggested timing and data collection.

Table 10. Proposed Implementation of Classroom Vibe Inquiry Cycle

When	Steps/Description
Mid Term 1	**Target Class** Choose **one** class upon which to focus your improvement effort. While it might be tempting to engage in this process with multiple classes, it can be challenging, so I recommended working with one class.
Mid-late Term 1	**Initial Diagnostic Data Collection** Choose a data collection strategy to collect evidence about your classroom practice. While several strategies have been mentioned, I recommend using a student perception of teaching survey. This is because I advise using the most objective and reliable form of evidence as to the basis for drawing inferences about improvement efforts.
Late Term 1	**Identify – Research – Establish – Plan** Use the data you have collected to identify your evidence-informed need. Based on this, spend some time doing some research before establishing your goal and putting together your plan of attack. Note: It can be helpful to do this stage with a peer or instructional coach.
Term 2 & Term 3	**Enact – Review – Refine – Re-enact** This phase is effectively where the rubber hits the road. It is about making changes to your classroom practice, seeking formative feedback to help you reviewing or evaluate the effectiveness of changes you are making and finally make refinements. I recommend using self-reflection, micro-teaching, or peer observation for data collection in this phase. Note: This cycle of review and refinement may occur several times.
Early Term 4	**Summative Data Collection** This phase is about collecting data that will allow you to reflect upon and evaluate the impact of your improvement efforts. Again, while several strategies have been mentioned, I recommend using a student perception of teaching survey.
Mid Term 4	**Evaluate** This phase focuses on examining the summative data collected in conjunction with evidence collected throughout the entire improvement journey. The goal is to celebrate your efforts and evaluate the effectiveness of changes you have made so you can decide if further improvement is possible or if you can move onto your next improvement effort.

CHAPTER SUMMARY – ENHANCING YOUR CLASSROOM VIBE

This chapter has focused on outlining a practical process of inquiry by which a teacher can seek evidence of their classroom vibe and subsequently engage in improvements. This process has included using a variety of strategies to collect evidence regarding the status of your classroom vibe. Further, we considered a series of frameworks to help you set specific goals, plan for their implementation, and evaluate their impact.

Figure 9. Amplifying Improvement with Feedback

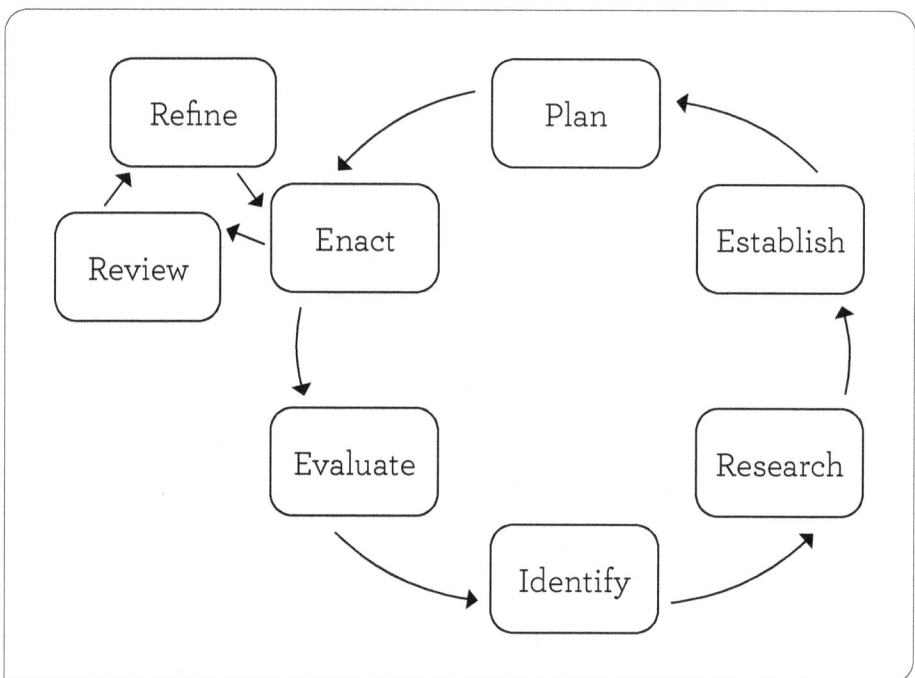

REFLECTION QUESTIONS

Take some time to reflect on and answer each of these questions. Make notes or draw pictures.

Do whatever helps you process the ideas and concepts discussed, and if you feel comfortable, share your answers with a colleague.

- Do you collect evidence about your classroom practice?

- If yes, what evidence have you collected to help you understand the status of the vibe in your classrooms? What does it tell you? How have you used it to inform improvement efforts?

- If no, why not? What support do you need to get started? Who do you need to seek help from to get started?

CHAPTER 3

Enhancing Teacher Credibility

Figure 10. The Building Blocks of Teacher Credibility

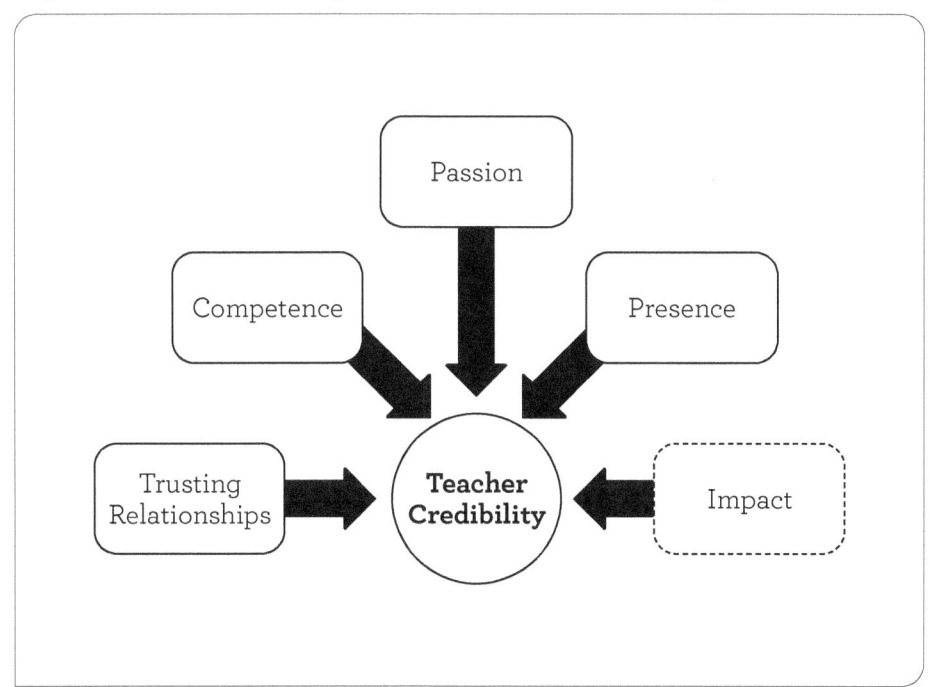

> **credibility** (kre-də-'bi-lə-tē)
> noun
>   "*the quality of being trusted and believed in.*"

LEARNING INTENTIONS

In this chapter, we will be delving a little deeper into Teacher Credibility. To do this, we will look in greater depth at the five elements of practice that contribute to a teacher's credibility. In addition, and perhaps most importantly, we will consider ideas for you to reflect on and integrate into your classroom practice to build credibility in the classroom and enhance your classroom's vibe.

By the conclusion of this chapter, you will:
- Be able to explain the features of teacher credibility and describe the areas of your practice upon which it is built.
- Be ready to start implementing new strategies in your classroom to enhance your teacher credibility.

In Chapter 1, we briefly identified that a teacher's credibility is about the belief or perceptions of their students that the teacher in question can positively impact their learning. Teacher credibility is, then, a powerful influence for teachers to consider to improve their practice, their classroom vibe, and their students' learning. Indeed, with an effect size of 1.09, there is clear evidence that if students see their teachers as credible, they believe that they are more likely to succeed and subsequently do.

Teacher Credibility is comprised of five interrelated factors. These include a teacher's:
- Capacity to building trusting, productive relationships.
- Competence as a leader of learning.
- Passion in the classroom.
- Presence and availability to support student learning.
- Capacity to impact upon student learning.

This chapter will describe these factors and provide practical strategies to support teachers in improving their classroom practice.

TRUSTING RELATIONSHIPS

Trust is fundamental to any successful and productive relationship, and teacher-student relationships are no different. As Thompson (1998, p. 6) has said:

> *"The most powerful weapon available to secondary teachers who want to foster a favorable learning climate is a positive relationship with our students."*

Further to this, enhancing student-teacher relationships can have long-lasting positive implications for students. This is because teachers who nurture trusting relationships with their students cultivate a vibe in their classrooms, facilitating a learning-focused atmosphere that is better placed to meet students' developmental, emotional, and academic needs (Rimm-Kaufman & Sandilos, 2010).

Ultimately, trust is about 'who you are' through the eyes of each of your students – it is about your actions, beliefs and ways of interacting.

If cultivating trusting relationships is something that you have decided to focus on improving in your classroom, then there are several principles to consider.

Principles for Nurturing Trust

- Make connections.
- Show them you believe so they can succeed.
- Be supportive and learn to listen.
- Be equitable and inclusive.
- Mind your manners.
- Allow for mistakes.

The following sections draw upon these principles and overview some simple strategies to help you nurture trusting relationships in your classroom.

Make Connections

Taking time to focus on building relationships with your students is critical to maximising classroom vibe; this is something that I wish that I had realised much earlier in my career. Making time to build relationships comes more naturally to some, but I can tell you that the effort is well worth it as students know if you are interested in them.

To build connections with your students, it is essential to make sure you quickly learn their names and use them. It also helps if you take the time to connect with them at every possible opportunity. For example, engage with them when they arrive at class, when you are moving around the classroom, and when you see them off as they leave, even outside of the classroom during recess or lunch. Also, when you are engaging with your students, it is important to balance the nature of your interactions with them. A model to keep in mind is positive interactions to every negative which has evolved out of Gottman and colleagues' (1998) work on marital happiness and stability.

On top of building relationships with your students, another powerful influence on your classroom vibe is to support your students to build relationships amongst themselves – think classroom cohesion. To do this, look for authentic opportunities for them to get to know each other and collaborate. When planning collaboration, it is essential to provide opportunities that are not simply cooperation but require interdependence.

One common exercise that can help break down barriers between students include is the good old icebreaker! As I am sure you know, icebreakers are typically fun activities that can break that ice by melting social barriers to help students feel more comfortable. They are often run at the beginning of a school year or class as they are great for making people feel comfortable when meeting a new group. They can also enhance social interaction. A classic experiment attributed to the Harvard Business School Professor Michael Norton highlighted the power of icebreaker activities. His study involved 221 individuals broken up into small teams of between two and four individuals who were asked to do a scavenger hunt task. They had to run across the campus and take selfies in front of various locations, and groups were allocated points for the number of photos taken in 45 minutes. There was no difference between the groups other than that half of the groups were asked to do an icebreaker activity when starting, the other half were not. The icebreaker activity the students were asked to do was actually quite basic – they were asked to stomp rhythmically and shout, "Let's go!". After the scavenger hunt, those groups who had completed the icebreaker had, on average, taken more photos than the other groups; they were also more likely to report liking their teammates. Pretty powerful finding really for a straightforward activity.

One possible activity to help students build connections and create the foundations for a collaborative learning environment is called *Marooned*; I vividly remember the power of this activity from my time in primary school. The premise for this activity is simple – your students are to use their creativity to imagine they are stranded on a desert island. The instructions are straightforward. Firstly, you need to break your class into small groups of perhaps four or five students. Then you need to ask them to imagine being stranded on a desert island in the Pacific Ocean. With this firmly in mind, their task is to use their ingenuity to choose items from their possessions at school to help them survive. Each student needs to contribute only one thing. Give the class 10-15 minutes to look through their belongings to choose an item. Finally, have each group share what they selected and explain how each object is essential. As an extension, ask the students to think of one item they would bring from home.

Another great activity to help students build connections is called *Getting-to-Know-You Bingo*. This activity has the goal of encouraging students to move about while getting to know their classmates. Again, the instructions are relatively simple. Hand each student a bingo card with a different descriptive sentence written in each square. Ask students to move about the room talking to their classmates. When they find a peer who fits a description, tell them to write the name in that specific box. Once a student has a name for every box, they call out, "Bingo!"

And finally, no discussion about icebreaker activities would be complete with the classic *Two Truths and One Lie*. This activity is timeless and works well when students don't know much about each other – at the beginning of the year is ideal. To start, you can model by sharing three 'facts' about you and explain that two are true and one is false, and then ask students to guess which is which. You can then ask students to write down their statements to share and take turns guessing each other's lies. This might occur in pairs, small groups, or with the entire class.

In addition to icebreaker activities, which are perfect for the start of the year or class, other activities to consider throughout the year include:

Sharing reflections
A powerful way to build relationships between your students is to run a brief weekly reflection session during which you ask students to write about a recent experience in their lives; it might be positive, negative, funny, or sad – anything they are prepared to share. Next, they can share with a small group of peers. These types of activities can be a great way to build social capital in your classroom (Reis et al., 2010).

Keeping a diary
Having been a full-time teacher, I know just how hard it can be to find time to regularly talk with students one-on-one. A great way to address this challenge, and establish a deeper connection with your students, is to allocate time for them to write a diary or reflection that they share with you. Your students can use this as an opportunity to write about themselves, their goals, what is going on in their lives, and how their learning is going. You can also respond with your encouragement and support. It is essential to remember that a task like this is about building communication between teacher and student, and you should avoid the temptation to make corrections. If they don't want to write a diary, perhaps they could draw a picture or create a poem or song to communicate about themselves to you.

Showing persistence

From my perspective, one of the key points raised in Chapter 1 is that our students experience us and our classrooms in different ways. Indeed, two students can concurrently have positive and negative experiences of our classroom simultaneously – this is important to remember, always. Further, I would argue that one of our responsibilities as teachers is to minimise this variation in student experience. This can be challenging, though, as there are always some students with whom we seem to build rapport more effortlessly and others with whom the process can take longer. Don't stress, this is normal. After all, we are all human. That said, it is our responsibility as teachers not just to be drawn to those students with whom connection is easier but to persist will ALL our students.

As I said earlier, every one of our students deserves to have positive experiences in our classrooms, and we teachers, as the adults in the room, have the moral imperative to take ownership of this through the deliberate, intentional relationships that we seek to nurture. This is a critical point because while it might be difficult to form connections with some students, we do not know what is happening in their lives. They may be suffering from anxiety or have faced some type of trauma, and your support could be the very help they need; it is very often those kids with whom it is most difficult to connect who are the students who need us the most.

Show Them You Believe So They Can Succeed

> *When teachers have high expectations for ALL students, communicate those expectations, and provide the support necessary to achieve them, student performance soars.*[5]

The expectations that we have for the learning of each of our students are critical. There are several reasons for this. First and foremost, this is because what we expect influences our students' outcomes. Indeed, research by academics such as Korp (2012) has shown that students can perceive our expectations and that these expectations can impact their academic experiences and outcomes. This is, of course, great when we have high expectations but is not optimal when expectations fall below what our students are capable of achieving. These sorts of outcomes are what we know as self-fulfilling prophecies and are the results of a process by which an originally false expectation can lead to its own confirmation; the Pygmalion effect described by Rosenthal and Jacobson (1968) is perhaps the most well-known example of this phenomenon. A recent example of this was the study conducted by Gentrup, Lorenz, Kristen, and Kogan (2020); they highlighted that while teacher expectations for students were not always accurate, their expectations were predictive of students' end-of-year achievements. This finding is consistent with the work of Rubie-Davies (2015), which has shown that students with teachers who hold high expectations for them tend to make larger academic gains and maintain a positive attitude towards themselves and their learning. In contrast, students whose teachers hold lower expectations have academic gains that are less pronounced and tend to hold more negative views of themselves.

Given the power of teacher expectations, what this means is that we should first seek to understand our students well enough to ensure that we hold appropriately high and challenging expectations for all of them. Secondly, we must strive to manage ourselves and our interactions and engagement with our students to communicate expectations effectively.

A great strategy to consider supporting you in demonstrating your belief in your students' capacity to achieve and succeed is to focus on both effort and growth over pure achievement. Yes, of course, student achievement is important. Of course, we want every student to achieve the highest standard possible. But given the diverse range of students in our classes regarding their prior achievement, motivation, and engagement, this means that potentially not every child will achieve at the same high standard in every topic. That said, every student is capable of both applying themselves to the best of their ability and also demonstrating growth both at and beyond reasonable expectations. In my mind, we should privilege application and growth as the primary focus of our expectations; this is essentially the gist of Carol Dweck's (2008) work *Mindset* and Angela Duckworth's (2016) work *Grit*.

Be Supportive and Learn to Listen

Listening is a necessary starting point of any positive and respectful relationship. In fact, as a source of building trust, listening is one of the most powerful ways of showing students that you respect them; showing that you have listened through your actions cements the deal.

Two related strategies worth considering include active listening and active constructive responding.

Active listening is perhaps best described as a way of listening with all five senses. It requires listeners to be fully concentrating on what is being said by a speaker. It also necessitates being seen to listen using both verbal and non-verbal messages, including eye contact, head nodding, smiling, and agreeing (by saying 'Yes' or simply 'Mmm hmm') to both demonstrate engagement and provide encouragement.

Active constructive responding is a way of responding when someone shares good news or experiences. Active constructive responding is a powerful strategy as it can indicate that the listener finds both the shared experience and relationship important and valuable. Active constructive responding literally involves responding with interest and enthusiasm by asking questions that help a person almost re-live the moment. It can also be further enhanced through body language, such as leaning into the conversation and movement or hand gestures.

In addition, another powerful strategy for building a classroom's vibe is by making sure that you take the time to talk with your students about their learning and experience at school in general, not just in your subject and classroom. For example, Delamont and Galton (1986) showed that in high school, if a teacher talks with a student for only 15 or more minutes about their learning across all of their subjects, then they are more likely to recall your support. This is not particularly surprising as it would rarely happen – think back, can you remember any teachers who took this level of interest in your learning? How many people take this level of interest in you now as an adult?

Be Equitable and Inclusive

As teachers, we need to be aware that if we do not recognise each of our student's capabilities and voices, we risk communicating a lack of confidence in their abilities. This is not good, as students may disengage if they perceive that we do not expect that they can contribute to a class's learning through discussion or answering a question. This can be further exacerbated if a student feels that the participation of other students is privileged over them by being called upon more regularly. This means that we need to be mindful and use strategies to make sure we call on all students equally.

A great classic approach to doing this focuses on being truly random by keeping a tub or jar of icy-pole sticks, one with each student's name on it, near your desk and drawing one randomly as required. You could also achieve this by writing your students' names on a list with a number next to them and then select a student to ask by rolling two dice. Alternatively, you might look to a higher tech option such as the Random Name Picker <https://miniwebtool.com/random-name-picker/> or Wheel of Names <https://WheelOfNames.com>.

Please note that when using an approach like this, it is important to ensure that your students appreciate the benefits. This means that you need to let them know why you are doing it. There are, of course, many reasons why you might use this approach. For example, to ensure that all students have a voice and the opportunity to share their knowledge and perspectives. Or to ensure that those students who often try to avoid contributing are involved. No matter your reasons, it is important to ensure that you nurture a safe space for students by letting them know that it is okay to pass if they do not know an answer or feel uncomfortable. Also, if your students are genuinely anxious about being put on the spot in front of their peers, it is important to provide an option to opt-out of the process until they are more comfortable. To truly keep your students on their toes, you might deviate from time to time and call on a student who you notice has been off task.

Mind Your Manners

Whether we like it or not, our students are vigilant observers of how we interact with them and others. This is important to remember as it can impact the nature of our relationships with them. It is critical, then, to consider how we engage with our students and other individuals more generally at school. Central to this is being mindful of managing our emotions as our students notice both the positive and negative approaches that we use. For instance, they pay attention to how we regulate ourselves in class or show an openness to talk about our frustrations. Unfortunately, they also notice damaging strategies, such as yelling, not listening, or making disrespectful comments (see Jones, Bouffard & Weissbourd, 2013).

This means we need to bring mindfulness into our classrooms to ensure that we engage as our best possible selves. Roeser and colleagues (2012) have described this as teachers needing to bring a powerful set of "habits of mind" including awareness, attention, flexibility, and intentionality into their practice.

Allow for Mistakes

Making mistakes is a necessary part of the learning process and a prerequisite for success. Like Michael Jordan, perhaps the greatest basketball player the world has seen once said:

> *I've missed more than 9000 shots in my career. I've lost almost 300 games. Twenty-six times I've been trusted to take the game-winning shot and missed. I've failed over, and over, and over again in my life. And that is why I succeed.*

More than being wrong, mistake-making can stimulate learning. Indeed, feedback, a known high-impact strategy, thrives on errors and misconceptions. Carol Dweck, whose work has focused on the psychology of mindset, has encouraged teachers to build cultures of "embraced mistakes" in their classrooms. Indeed, when students perceived their classroom as mistake-friendly, they increased their effort and learning. The lesson for teachers is that constructing a classroom culture in which mistakes are considered positive can improve learning.

Central to establishing a mistake-friendly culture in the classroom is considering how we as teachers respond to mistakes. Critically, mistakes must lead to productive, positive conversations about where to next and must never lead to shame or disapproval.

To begin cultivating a mistake-friendly environment, consider the following suggestions.

You might include a 'mistake of the day' in your classes by making mistakes, on purpose, for students to notice. Give your students a heads up in advance, so they are paying attention. Once your students see the errors, challenge them to explain what is wrong and to correct them. A positive outcome of this can be the development of reasoning skills.

Let your students in on the power of mistakes and help them to recognise that they are powerful learning opportunities that have led to some of humanity's most significant accomplishments. Alexander Fleming's discovery of penicillin is a good example. The reason he made the discovery is that he didn't clean up before going on holiday. After returning, he cleaned the petri dishes he left at his desk and noticed one covered in colonies of bacteria, except in one place where mould was growing. He investigated and discovered that the mould could kill a wide range of bacteria, therefore discovering penicillin. The take-away is that mistakes can be potent so try to help your students understand this. To support this, here are some famous quotes about the power of mistakes.

The Power of Mistakes

Anyone who has never made a mistake has never tried anything new.

Albert Einstein

If you're not prepared to be wrong, you'll never come up with anything original.

Sir Ken Robinson

It's not a person's mistakes which define them – it's the way they make amends.

Freya North

If I find 10,000 ways something won't work, I haven't failed. I am not discouraged, because every wrong attempt discarded is another step forward.

Thomas A. Edison

Sometimes when you innovate, you make mistakes. It is best to admit them quickly, and get on with improving your other innovations.

Steve Jobs

Everyone makes mistakes. The important thing is to not make the same mistake twice..

Stephanie Perkins

An inventor fails 999 times, and if he succeeds once, he's in. He treats his failures simply as practice shots.

Charles F. Kettering

Show me a person who has never made a mistake and I'll show you someone who has never achieved much.

Joan Collins

Also consider the ideas that sit behind Barney Saltzberg's book *Beautiful Oops*, which focuses on accepting, celebrating, building upon, and learning from our mistakes. In our classes, it is therefore essential to provide opportunities for students to do this. One way might be to initiate a conversation or lessons with your students about the power of mistakes. You could do this by sharing either some of the more famous mistakes listed in the previous section or errors that you made that have created powerful learning. After this, you can use the following questions as a series of discussion prompts:

- *Have you ever made a mistake? What happened?*
- *How did making a mistake make you feel?*
- *How did you react after making a mistake?*
- *How have you reacted after seeing a classmate or friend make a mistake?*
- *How might we behave differently so that we are more optimistic with ourselves and our classmates when we make mistakes?*
- *How might this help us be less tense, anxious, and open to learning?*
- *Can you think of a time when making mistakes would be okay?*

As a fourth option, you might look to set tasks that provide your students with opportunities to make mistakes. For example, set your students a challenging open-ended question – and then stand back and let them investigate. It can, of course, be tough not to intervene when we can see students struggling, going off track, or setting themselves up to fail. But our students need the opportunity to feel this challenge. These are the situations when they are deep in what Nottingham (2017) describes as the Learning Pit, and if we intervene too soon, we rob them of the opportunity to learn. As they engage in these types of learning processes, making mistakes, it is essential to remind them that these mistakes are a necessary and fundamental part of the learning process and a significant opportunity for learning that they should embrace.

COMPETENCE

For students to perceive a teacher as competent, their teacher must exude the confidence to teach their subject area and demonstrate the capability to deliver it in a meaningful and engaging manner. This is more than simply having subject matter knowledge though. While, of course, subject matter expertise does have an overall positive impact on student learning, there are far more important considerations, such as how to most effectively teach a subject and use the most appropriate routines to manage and engage your class. Sadly, this is something I had to learn the hard way early in my career.

If building your students' perceptions of your teacher competence is a goal, there are several principles to consider.

Principles for Demonstrating Competence

- Be prepared.
- Know what to teach and how to teach it.
- Confidence is critical.
- Run a tight ship.
- Keep your trains on time.

The following sections draw upon these principles and overview some simple strategies to help you nurture perceptions about teacher competence in your classroom.

Be Prepared

As they say, Proper Planning Prevents Poor Performance. One of the most effective strategies to ensure your students perceive you as a competent teacher is to prepare for each lesson properly. Seems pretty logical and straightforward, right? But I can tell you, I have heard plenty of teachers jokingly refer to being but one step or lesson in front of their students. The reality is that it is more complex than being one step or even one lesson ahead. This is because being properly prepared involves a great many steps. These steps include:
1. Thinking through learning intentions and success criteria for a lesson;
2. Identifying the strategies and skills your students will need to meet the success criteria;
3. Planning your assessment strategies;
4. Thinking through pacing; planning worked examples and activities;
5. Planning the types of questions, you will want to ask students; and
6. Thinking through potential student misconceptions, the kinds of questions they might ask, and how you will deal with them.

As I said, this is undoubtedly not just staying one step ahead – nor can it be achieved by following the 3-step planning process (i.e., the final three steps before entering your classroom). If you are a recently graduated teacher, I can promise, though, that time spent thinking through these things earlier in your career will pay you back in spades later in your career; take it from a relatively old hand. Also, if possible, I advise planning collaboratively with other teachers – as they say, two heads are better than one.

Know What To Teach and How To Teach It

To be a teacher, it is impactful to command the subject or material you teach. But to be a teacher with credibility, you need so much more. In addition to knowing what to teach, you also need to know the how. This powerful combination of understanding both the 'what' and 'how' to teach is what Shulman (1987) called pedagogical content knowledge, and it is a prerequisite for effective teachers. This is because such knowledge empowers teachers, equipping them with the two key things. Firstly, the content knowledge for their subject including a diverse range of factual knowledge of their subject combined with a deep conceptual understanding of the critical theoretical aspects and big ideas. And, secondly, an appreciation of how to teach their subject, including an understanding of how learning in their subject progresses, likely student misconceptions, their possible causes, and necessary interventions combined.

Knowledge of all this means that a teacher is better equipped to plan for the developmental needs of each of their students, respond moment-by-moment to their needs, diagnose and remediate misconceptions, invite inquiry and discussion by students, and evaluate student learning. Several ideas for building pedagogical content knowledge will be discussed in the next section.

Confidence Is Critical

Self-confidence in the classroom and teaching ability are closely related. A helpful way of thinking about enhancing self-efficacy in the classroom is based on Freeman's (1989) model of teaching, which described teaching as a decision-making process drawing upon teacher knowledge, skill, attitude, and awareness. Drawing upon these, Valazza (nd) proposed four key improvement areas for teachers: professional knowledge, reflective practice, self-knowledge, and attitude. I have integrated these further to present four options for building teacher confidence: enhancing teacher professional knowledge, capacity to engage in reflective practice, self-awareness, and understanding impact.

As teachers, we can enhance our self-confidence by building professional knowledge. These days this can be a relatively simple task as there are many options available to help. For example, professional associations can play a pivotal role in supporting professional growth, with many having publications that support the development of subject matter and pedagogical knowledge. They also often offer training sessions and conferences that can support growth. Nowadays, social media creates an ocean of opportunity, with many subject-specific TeachMeets regularly organised by teachers online and face-to-face. Online discussion groups, blogs, podcasts, Facebook pages, and LinkedIn groups also offer great opportunities for teachers to share tips of the trade. To get started, all you need to do is hop on Google and start searching; I spent an hour this afternoon in a group discussion on education research hosted on LinkedIn.

In looking to build and deepen professional knowledge, I would also look for opportunities to engage in collaborative discussion within your school and find people to learn from through formal or informal mentoring. Whether they know it or not, my career was shaped by four or five key people I connected with and learned from; I am fortunate enough to call many of these people my friends still today.

A second option for building confidence in the classroom is through engaging in reflective practice. This means being open to experimenting with your classroom practice, reflecting on its impact and effectiveness, and drawing on the experience to improve even further. I can attest that taking such an approach is beneficial. Additionally, I would argue that exploring new strategies can make teaching more engaging, which can also help maintain and improve passion for teaching. Such exploration would fit nicely within the active inquiry process that this book advocates for teachers to engage in, to enhance the vibe they cultivate in their classrooms.

Thirdly, linked to this idea of reflective practice is the notion that improving in an activity requires having a high degree of self-knowledge. Teachers can enhance their self-awareness by reflecting on the following:

> *What kind of teacher am I?*
> *How do my students perceive me?*
> *How do my colleagues perceive me?*
> *What are my strengths and weakness?*
> *What do I need to do to improve?*

These questions all link to the inquiry model I have advocated for in Chapter 3.

Another opportunity I see for building a teacher's confidence is through recognising and celebrating success. For me, this is about seeking evidence of our impact on students' learning outcomes and experiences in the classroom. For example, you might examine pre- and post-test data to understand how much your students have learned during a topic. This can also be a great way to understand what your students know at the beginning of a unit of work and can help you identify what you need to do next with your class at the conclusion. If looking at test scores is not your preference, you might also look to artefacts of student work overtime to see changes in the quality of the work they are producing. You can also keep track of how your students are engaging and interacting in class, the types of questions they ask, and their attendance. The possibilities are endless!

Run a Tight Ship

> *When teachers have high expectations for ALL students, communicate those expectations, and provide the support necessary to achieve them, student performance soars.*[6]

When I think about expectations that we need to map out for our students, I am thinking about two distinct but related types of expectations. The first is expectations for the learning in class. The second is expectations for behaviour and engagement in class. I address expectations for learning in other sections of the book (see Show Them You Believe So They Can Achieve in Chapter 3 and Map Out the Learning in Chapter 4). The second type, expectations of behaviour, we will address now.

Behavioural expectations are those that relate to the protocol or rules that keep a class running. Communicating clear classroom behavioural expectations to your student is essential as it has been shown to make concentrating and teaching in the classroom easier. Further, classrooms with clear behavioural expectations experience nearly 30% fewer disruptions than classrooms where expectations have not been established. It should be apparent, then, that setting clear expectations for student behaviour is an essential task for teachers to prime students for what is about to be learned and how it is to be learned.

Simply announcing expectations or rules for a classroom is insufficient to instil or curb specific behaviours. I would argue, actually, that expectations should not simply be imposed on students but rather co-constructed with them. In fact, student involvement increases their sense of ownership and the likelihood of making the expectations their own and taking responsibility for their learning and behaviour. This is critically important for nurturing a classroom's vibe. As Erwin (2004) has said, when a teacher engages the students in developing clear behavioural guidelines that the students see as adding quality to their school lives, the relationship between the students and the teacher is enhanced.

So how might you co-construct behavioural guidelines with your students?

As I am sure you can appreciate, developing behavioural guidelines is not a process that students are likely to see as 'fun'. That said, there are strategies for involving students that might be helpful. For example:

Seven Steps to Student Sanity

Step 1
Start a class discussion by asking your class one or all of the following questions:
- What do you think should and shouldn't be allowed in the classroom? Why?
- What makes a well-managed classroom? What should learning look like?
- What did you see the teacher and students doing?

Step 2
Give your students time to talk in groups before reporting their ideas back to the class. This opportunity creates a chance to gain insights into your class and prime them for the next step.

Step 3
Ask your students to make suggestions for behavioural expectations via a group discussion. For this step, ask for a volunteer or voluntell a student to act as a scribe for— let them know that all ideas should be written in each student's actual words.

Step 4
Once your students' ideas are exhausted, with all suggestions listed, ask your class to review them and decide if any might be collapsed into a single expectation or discarded. This is also an excellent time to ask your students to think about whether the list might be reorganised or grouped into three to five expectations under different headings.

Step 5
Lead a final discussion with your students to finalise the rules.

Step 6
Share the guidelines in a place for all students to see.

Step 7
Once a class has created their behavioural expectations, you need to plan for their enactment. To do this, you might use discussions or role-playing to unpack what expectations should look, sound, and feel like in action. It might also be a good idea to have students commit to upholding the guidelines.

Note: The process of co-constructing behavioural guidelines to communicate expectations can take time to complete, but it is well worth it. If you choose to engage in this process, make sure you do so at the beginning of the school year for the best impact. A final consideration is that over time your students will inevitably begin to ignore or test the expectations. When this happens, it is essential to take time to review and recommit to the rules.

Once you have your expectations in place and you need to correct students for inappropriate choices, it is important to do so in a constructive manner. Indeed, as I have learned through the years, it is possible to discipline students and build positive relationships at the same time. For example, when you need to speak to a student about their behaviour or work ethic, try to do so discreetly, such as before or after class time. This is because creating a situation in which a student feels publicly embarrassed or humiliated can very quickly destroy any established trust. It is also worth being honest about the impact that their behaviour has on the learning of others.

Boynton and Boynton (2015) have overviewed a process that allows you to correct a student while also ensuring they can maintain their dignity and therefore increase the likelihood they will reflect on their actions and behaviour and make better choices in the future. Their process offers eight simple steps to provide quick, fair, and meaningful consequences for inappropriate behaviours while communicating care and respect for the student.

1. Review the inappropriate behaviour.
2. Identify and acknowledge the student's feelings.
3. Review alternate actions and behaviours.
4. Explain the relevant school or classroom policy or rules as they apply to the situation.
5. Remind the student that expectations for all students are the same.
6. Tell the student that you are disappointed in their actions and that you must apply a consequence for their action.
7. Outline an immediate and suitable consequence.
8. Communicate the expectation that in the future, the student will make better choices.

Be firm but fair
An important consideration for the construction and enactment of behavioural guidelines is the notion of fairness. Over the years, many student surveys have shown that fairness is one of the most frequently desired qualities they hope for in a teacher. Indeed, for students to trust their teachers, they must perceive them to have a firm yet fair approach to classroom management. But what does this mean?

To ensure your students perceive you as having a firm yet fair approach to classroom management, you need to establish clear expectations in your class for both behaviour and learning. It is also essential that once you have defined your expectations that you are consistent in their application.

This is because if your students perceive you as inconsistent, it can erode the trust and vibe of your classroom. In setting out classroom rules, it is worth considering co-constructing rules with your students so they are equal participants in setting their climate of respect and responsibility. We will talk a little more about expectations for behaviour and learning a little later.

Does fair mean equal?

An essential quality in a teacher is that of fairness. But what is fair, and what does it mean to be fair? Fairness can be defined as treating everyone the same. Given that students are not the same, though, it could be argued that treating all students equally is the most unfair way of treating them; we must help our students understand this. You can also introduce examples of how you intend to be fair but not necessarily equal.

Keep Your Trains on Time

In his paper, Carroll (1963) connected learning to time, proposing that what he called *true learning* is contingent upon the actual time a student spends engaged in the process of learning. As we will see, this is much more than keeping students busy, 'doing' things in class. Indeed, subsequent research investigated the effective use of classroom time, identifying practices and strategies that contribute to student learning. For instance, the Californian Beginning Teacher Evaluation Study (BTES) (Fisher et al., 1978) highlighted teaching practices and classroom conditions that support student learning. They also identified three ideas about time relating to effective learning, including allocated time, engaged time, and academic learning time.

Firstly, allocated time was conceptualised as the total time available for learning to occur, for example, the length of a class or the school day. This was considered to represent our students 'opportunity to learn'. The BTES showed that students achieve to a higher level when their teachers allocate more time to a specific content area.

Secondly, engaged time was defined as the time students spend actively engaged in learning tasks. The BTES found that the greater the engaged time, the better students achieved. The BTES also showed that instructional styles that were more interactive resulted in higher levels of engaged time, resulting in increased student learning. There are many interactive strategies available; I describe three below and have included several more in Table 11.

Firstly, *Think-Pair-Share* is a classic strategy to engage students. To use this approach, you ask students to follow three steps. The first is to have them THINK about what they have read/heard/learned. Secondly, ask them to turn to a partner or PAIR and SHARE their thinking. And then finally, you might follow up with an opportunity for each group to share key points or reflections from their discussion back to the class.

Another great interactive strategy is called *Q&A*. To use this strategy, take a few moments before beginning a lesson to give your students a brief overview of the topic to be covered. Then ask them to let you know any burning questions that might have occurred to them or anything which has made them curious. Note them down on the board, or if you feel technology-savvy, try using a digital platform such as Padlet to capture their questions and comments. Once questions have been collected, you can then use them to inform how you deliver your lesson. For instance, you might choose to pause throughout your class to address student-generated questions, or you might elect to spend more time on certain areas throughout the lesson.

Another good interactive strategy you might like to consider is the *Jigsaw Method*, a cooperative learning technique developed by Emeritus Professor Elliot Aronson from the University of California, Santa Cruz. The purpose of the method is to enable each member of a 'home' group of students to specialise and become an expert in one element of a topic they are studying to support their 'home' group to complete a shared learning task. For example, you might be learning about desert habitats, and the elements of expertise might include desert plants, soil types, desert animals, and so on. Students meet up with the other students that have been assigned to their element to become experts. After this, all students return to their 'home' group to bring back their expert knowledge so that the shared learning task can be completed. For more information about the Jigsaw Method, go to <www.jigsaw.org>.

Table 11. Further Examples of Interactive Teaching Strategies

Buzz Session Break students up into small groups. Assign each group a specific problem to solve or task to undertake. Ask each group to monitor and regulate their collaboration and ask them to share their findings with the class.
Case Study Break your class into small groups and give each group an open-ended scenario or a real-life problem requiring analysis, discussion, drawing conclusions, making recommendations, or proposing a solution. Make sure you give your students an appropriate amount of time (i.e., a class, a week, a term) and then have groups deliver a presentation to overview their report.
Be Random As mentioned earlier, it can be a powerful motivator for students to know they might be called on randomly to answer a question, so try one of the methods described on pages 56–57.

And, finally, academic learning time was considered to be about the quality of learning time and is the total time students spend actively engaged in learning, working on learning tasks that are appropriately challenging, and being successful. The principle is that when instruction is targeted by a teacher so that their students are more often successful than not (i.e., successful three-quarters of the time), students tend to be more engaged and achieve at higher levels. Students love to be challenged, and for those who do not, we need to set more appropriate challenges to draw them in and ensure they exceed their personal bests. To ensure maximum academic learning time in class, there are steps that teachers can take, as outlined in Figure 11 below.

Figure 11. Steps to Maximising Academic Learning Time in Class

---

1. Understand the range of student attainment in their classes

In the sections *Create Appropriate Challenge* on page 84 and *Connect the New with the Old* on page 104 you will find useful appropriate strategies to support this.

2. Targeted teaching and learning

See sections *Check for Understanding* on page 102 and *Connect the New with the Old* on page 104.

3. Ensure engaging lessons

See *Explanation* starting on page 87.

4. Ensure supportive engagement and interaction in class

See section *Make Connections* on pages 51–54.

PASSION

Teacher Passion is about the enthusiasm a teacher brings to their classroom combined with their capability to communicate and transmit this enthusiasm to their students. Passion is an essential ingredient for effective teaching and a classroom's vibe. Indeed, Haskins (2000) has stressed the importance for teachers to both appear as in control of their classrooms and to be energised by them. He went on to impress the disastrous potential of appearing the opposite, indicating that the outcome would be rapid evaporation of any excitement or enthusiasm students might have had for the class and its content.

Passionate teachers, therefore, have a significant impact on their students and their learning (Hattie, 2009). Their beliefs and enthusiasm help us recognise our own inner values and turn us on to be excited and involved in the learnings of their subject. Further, Keller et al. (2014) showed that what they called dispositional teacher enthusiasm directly correlates with student interest in their subject, with subsequent findings suggesting that this link is due to students' heightened perceptions of their teacher's enthusiasm. In other words, more enthusiastic teachers are perceived as such, which positively impacts their students' motivation to achieve. Remember your most impactful teacher – they wanted to turn you onto their passion.

If passion in your classrooms is something you have decided to focus on improving, there are several principles to consider.

Principles for Demonstrating Passion

- Be infectious and share your passion.
- Delivery is key.
- Focus on you.
- Build their passion.

The following sections draw upon these principles to overview some simple strategies to help you nurture perceptions about teacher passion in your classroom.

Be Infectious and Share Your Passion

On the basis that passion can seem infectious, then we, as teachers, must be, or at the very least must appear to be, passionate and energetic about what we teach. Indeed, as Gilal and colleagues (2019) have shown, when we show passion in and through our teaching, our students feel it, and we draw them into the lessons and motivate them.

It is true, of course, that sometimes we might not be excited about what we are teaching, but teaching does often involve acting (although whenever possible, authenticity always wins). It is okay, of course, not to be inwardly excited about everything you teach every day. I was a high school mathematics teacher, and there were the odd few days that quadratic equations didn't always float my boat. This is okay but be mindful never of letting negative messages creep into your teaching as students will pick it up and take it on board, and their views of what they are learning and potentially your subject will be tainted. So, when you are not feeling it, you might need to try a little 'fake it till you make it'.

Delivery is Key

Exactly how a message is conveyed to its intended audience goes a long way to nurturing the vibe in a classroom. From their analysis of data collected from 1,700 classrooms, Clinton and colleagues (2014) found that a teacher's delivery is more often than not counterproductive and does not support active learning. They found that teachers talk too fast, with language that is a year or more beyond the level of the students they were teaching. More than this, they were asking 150-200 questions per lesson, allowing less than three seconds response time per question. Remember, no one becomes a teacher to do a lousy job, so all of the above is unintentional; unfortunately, it excludes and exhausts students and means that the teacher is doing most of the work!

If enhancing delivery is an area you are interested to improve your classroom's vibe, several ideas to focus on include:
- Use a speaking style that uses minimal filler words, such as 'okay', 'you know', and 'umm', and vary your style by using elements of tone, pitch, speed, and inflection.
- Vary your physical movements (i.e., gestures, facial expressions, and eye contact).
- Try different ways of interaction like story-telling, discussions, visual aids, technology, video, simulations, role-plays, and PowerPoint.
- Don't be afraid to use pauses and wait, allowing time for students to engage.

Focus on You

No matter their energy, a teacher cannot be inspiring all the time. Nor can they be inspiring if stressed or drained. Therefore, it is necessary to make time for yourself both in terms of your social and emotional well-being and your own learning, both professional and otherwise. Doing so will keep you both engaged as a teacher and might very well provide ideas and strategies to bring into your classroom. Indeed, Williams Jnr (2003), Past President of the Association for Supervision and Curriculum Development (ASCD), in his piece 'A Passion for Learning

Begins with a Spark', highlighted the power and importance of ongoing professional learning as well as personal reflection and renewal.

Build Their Passion

In addition to demonstrating your passion, supporting students to find and build their passion is a great way to enhance classroom vibe. This speaks to the often-cited W. B. Yeats quote:

> *Education is not the filling of a bucket but the lighting of a fire.*

For example, finding opportunities for your *students to share their passions can motivate* them and their peers. It is crucial to ensure there are norms in place so that sharing takes place in a safe space involving an absence of feedback or judgment. It can also be powerful to create opportunities for students to connect with peers who share the same passion. This is because it can serve as confirmation that their passion is valued and that they, as a person, are also valuable. It can also be powerful to create opportunities, through guest speakers, video presentations, or excursions, for students to experience firsthand passionate people. Even if students are not directly interested in the topic, they may benefit from seeing individuals express their passions.

IMMEDIACY/PRESENCE

Immediacy or presence as an aspect of Teacher Credibility is about how students perceive the positive, supportive presence of a teacher in the classroom. It is essential for nurturing your classroom vibe. Immediacy is about a teacher's capacity to break down perceived barriers between themselves and their pupils. Mehrabian's (1971) principle of immediacy says that people are drawn toward persons and things they like, evaluate highly, and prefer. In the context of teaching, immediacy is then about behaviours that bring students and teachers closer together. In the classroom, a teacher demonstrating immediacy leans in to help their students, removing barriers and the distance between themselves and their students. Immediacy or presence in the classroom is unquestionably important as it is related to many important student outcomes. These include:
- Affective learning (Pogue & Ahyun, 2006)
- Cognitive learning (Chesebro & McCroskey, 2001)
- Student motivation (Christophel, 1990)
- Attendance (Rocca, 2004)
- Engagement in learning (Rocca, 2004).

Additionally, immediacy is positively associated with student perceptions of teacher competence, caring, and trustworthiness (Thewatt, 1999).

Immediacy is critical for cultivating classroom vibe and can be built by focusing on two types of classroom presence, including verbal and non-verbal behaviours. If enhancing immediacy in your classroom is something that you have decided to focus on improving in your classroom, then I propose two principles to consider.

Principles for Demonstrating Presence

- Watch your words.
- Mind how you move.

The following sections draw upon these principles to overview some simple strategies to help you nurture immediacy in your classroom.

Watch Your Words: Verbal Communication

Verbal communication is about the use of words to express a message. Suggestions for using verbal communication to close the distance between teachers and learners include:
- Making sure you call students by their names.
- Using individual pronouns such as 'you', 'yours', 'I', 'me',and 'mine' can create space. Therefore, focus on collective pronouns such as 'we', 'us', and 'our'.
- Finding opportunities to talk with your students both in and out of class time; talk does not need to be solely focused on learning.
- Taking time to give feedback, one on one, to students; making sure that they hear, understand, and act accordingly.
- Taking time to ask students how they feel about things.
- Try limiting talk time to what is necessary and allow space for your students to talk more.

Mind How You Move: Non-Verbal Communication

Non-verbal communication involves body language and physical gestures to help convey a message. Possibilities for non-verbal communication strategies to close the distance between teachers and learners include:
- Looking and smiling at the class while talking and minimise the time looking at the board, your notes, or the floor.
- Moving around the classroom while teaching – not just standing up the front of your classroom or sitting behind your desk.

- Being physically expressive and use gestures when presenting.
- Removing or reducing physical barriers within the classroom that can get between you and your students. For example, get rid of rows in your classrooms and use clusters or a circle.
- Trying to look at ease by using a relaxed body position.
- Scanning the room to build connections by making eye contact with the entire class.
- When helping students one-on-one, sit with them.
- Avoid hovering over student conversations. Instead, lean and listen to those conversations.
- Don't interrupt student discussions – too often.
- When talking to students, put yourself at their level. This might mean sitting on the floor or at their desk with them.

IMPACT

Impact as a facet of teacher credibility and consequently a classroom's vibe is an addition that I have made. The idea is, of course, embedded across all elements of Teacher Credibility and Teacher Clarity, but I believe this inclusion needs to be made more explicit. This is for two key reasons. Firstly, as outlined previously, Teacher Credibility is about whether we, as educators, manage ourselves in a way that means we can persuade our students that they can be successful. Secondly, a classroom's vibe is defined as being the learning-focused atmosphere of the classroom as experienced by the students. The implication is that for classroom vibe to be present, the students who enter our classrooms need to know and understand our capacity to impact their learning. To ensure this, we need to help our students understand and appreciate the impact that we are having on their learning.

CHAPTER SUMMARY – BUILDING TEACHER CREDIBILITY

The key message from this chapter is that teacher credibility is an important consideration for teachers looking to build their classroom's vibe. Broadly speaking, the concept of teacher credibility is concerned with the beliefs students form about a teacher's capacity to impact their learning positively. More specifically, it is about their perceptions of the nature of relationships in the classroom, both between teacher and students and students and their trustworthiness, passion, and presence. Further, all of this is wrapped up in our students' perception that a teacher can and will positively impact their learning.

We have seen throughout this chapter many practical strategies that teachers can use to help build their *Teacher Credibility*.

REFLECTION QUESTIONS

Take some time to reflect on and answer each of these questions. Make notes or draw pictures.

Do whatever helps you process the ideas and concepts discussed, and if you feel comfortable, share your answers with a colleague.

- How would you describe Teacher Credibility to a colleague?

- How can building your Teacher Credibility enhance your classroom vibe?

- What resonated for you in this chapter? What challenged you?

- How would you describe the status of your Teacher Credibility with your students? What evidence do you have to support this?

- Following this chapter, what ideas or strategies can you commit to trialing in your classroom this week?

- What sort of obstacles can you foresee stopping you?

- What strategies can you plan to overcome these obstacles?

CHAPTER 4

Enhancing Teacher Clarity

Figure 12. The Building Blocks of Teacher Clarity

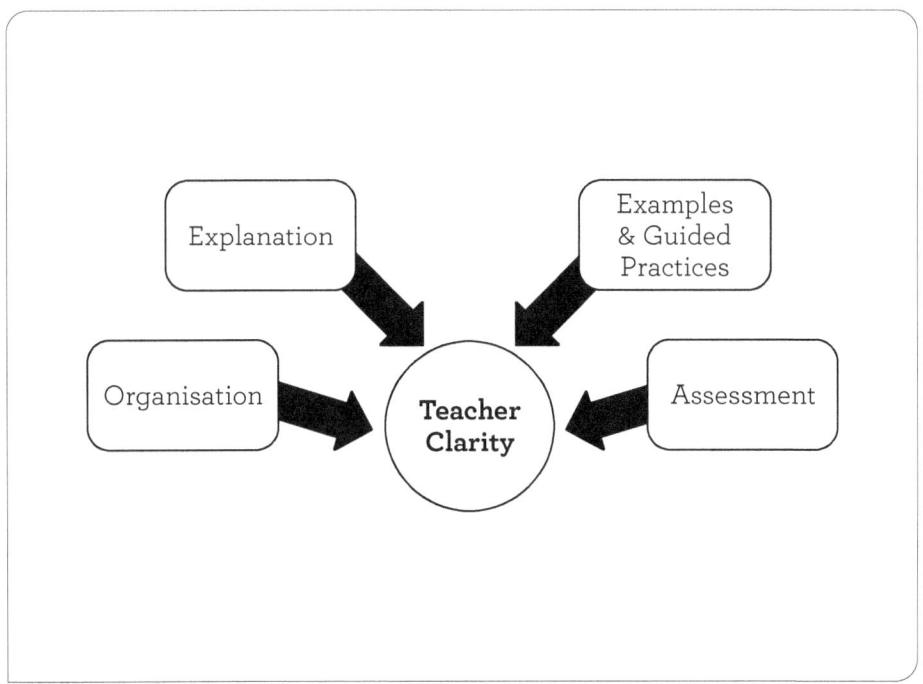

clarity (kler-ə-tē)
noun
> The quality of being expressed, remembered, understood.
> The quality of being easily seen or heard.

LEARNING INTENTIONS

In this chapter, we will delve a little deeper into Teacher Clarity. To do this, we will look in greater depth at the four elements of practice that contribute to a teacher's clarity. In addition, and perhaps most importantly, we will consider ideas and strategies for you to reflect on and integrate into your classroom practice to build clarity in the classroom and enhance your classroom's vibe.

By the conclusion of this chapter, you will:
- Be able to explain the features of teacher clarity and describe the areas of your practice upon which it is built.
- Be ready to start implementing new strategies in your classroom to enhance your teacher clarity.

As was identified earlier, a teacher's clarity is about the nature of communication between a teacher and their students. Teacher Clarity is not about whether a teacher speaks in a way that is easily understood. Instead, being a teacher with clarity means demonstrating complete confidence and understanding about what students are to learn in an upcoming unit of work before planning instruction and assessment and conveying this confidence to your students. As we have seen, the research shows us that Teacher Clarity is vital to ensuring students learn.

Teacher Clarity is comprised of four interrelated factors focused on a teacher's ability to:
- Organise student learning coherently.
- Introduce new learning.
- Support new learning with examples and guided practice.
- Embed a variety of assessment strategies effectively into practice.

Over the remainder of this chapter, a brief description of each of these factors will be provided. More importantly, though, practical strategies for enhancing each will be presented to support teachers in improving their classroom practice.

ORGANISATION

Clarity through organisation relates to whether lessons or a series of lessons are constructed logically. This does not mean that lessons need to be overly structured, as this can impede learning.

For a teacher to be perceived by their students as demonstrating organisation, they must incorporate elements of practice that streamline the lesson and enhance their students' learning. A prerequisite to this is that learning intentions are planned for, made transparent to students, and related to success criteria from the outset. Teaching must also be explicitly linked to the stated learning intentions and incorporate regular reviews of what has been learned in class. Teacher Clarity is more than just integrating these things into practice. For a teacher to genuinely demonstrate clarity through organisation, their students need to have clarity about what they are learning, where they are going, how it links with past learning, and what they need to do to succeed.

If enhancing clarity through organisation in your classroom is something you have decided to focus on improving, there are several principles to consider.

Principles for Showing Organisation

- Start with the why.
- Map out the learning.
- Create appropriate challenge.
- Build in time for review.

The following sections draw upon these principles to overview some simple strategies to help you nurture clarity through organisation in your classroom.

Start with the Why

When am I ever going to use this?

I have heard this phrase far too often throughout my career in education. Even as an educator of teachers. Therefore, helping students understand the relevance of what they are learning is an essential consideration for teachers. Indeed, to ensure engagement, our learners need to have some insight into why they are learning what is being taught, combined with understanding how it connects to previous learning, the real world, and future learning. This is what we call relevance.

For some subjects, demonstrating relevance is easy. For many subjects, it can be much more challenging for a teacher to make relevance obvious. For example, I am a mathematics teacher, and I can tell you that trying to convince Year 7 students about the relevance of long division was always a challenge. Further, it can be difficult for teachers to frame the importance of new knowledge and skills when they are merely links in the chain, so to speak, to learning that may occur in the future. In such instances, teachers need to help their students see the more immediate reason for their learning. Taking the time to do so is worth the trouble, though, as it not only fosters motivation, but it also deepens learning as students begin to make connections to larger concepts (Frey, Hattie & Fisher, 2018). Strategies that can help make current learning relevant include:

Help your students making connections
It is crucial to make an effort to explicitly draw your students' attention to how new learning links to past and future learnings. It is also powerful to help students understand how new learnings might be used outside of school as it can be very empowering for students to see the direct utility of knowledge and skills beyond the goal of passing or doing well in a subject.

Link lessons to learning
In some instances, it is necessary to make it utterly explicit that the real lesson is the learning skills and strategies being developed. For example, I have adapted an example task called the Algebra Attitude Adjustment, which overviews a great approach from an anonymous mathematics teacher that was outlined by Mendler (2014).

> **Algebra Attitude Adjustment**
>
> On the first day of the year, teacher Jordan Simons gives her mathematics class the Algebra Attitude Adjustment task. The introduction to the lesson begins with the provocation, "So, here you are, trapped, having to learn stuff you think you will never need!" It's all just so unfair! Jordan goes on to remind her students, even in the face of adversity, you should aspire to be positive, and a positive person would find a way to use a situation like this to their advantage – as the saying goes, they would take those lemons and make lemonade. Jordan finishes with, "So, here's the trick, the silver bullet, the secret to success. The key to surviving this class is that it isn't really about math or algebra. It is an opportunity to develop and practice the skills you need to be successful. So you should try and see it as a 'success' training class and remember while you may never use the mathematics skills again, you WILL use the problem-solving skills and learning strategies throughout your life again and again."

Map Out the Learning

Learning intentions are brief statements that describe what students should know, understand, or do as the result of teaching. Learning intentions are typically related to the curriculum, but they can also be outcomes that are beyond the scope of the documented curriculum. For example, learning intentions might focus upon Process Skills, Collaborative Skills, Social Skills, Learning Strategies, etc.

No matter the purpose of your lessons, it is critically important to make sure that their intended purpose is made explicitly clear to students. This is because without doing so, achieving success can feel a bit like a guessing game for students, where they must work out what we really want them to do to achieve, to what level and know the best ways of showing their learning. If you think about it, this just isn't fair.

Sharing learning intentions with students is a fundamental requirement for learning (Sadler, 1989). Indeed, if students understand the purpose of a lesson (or series of lessons), they learn more (see Clarke, 2021). Ensuring that you establish the purpose of a lesson is necessary to give your students the best chance of successful learning. Further, when teachers state their purpose for a lesson, they make their expectations for learning (and behaviour) clear. This is important because when teachers communicate their expectations and provide the necessary support, student outcomes are enhanced (Marzano, 2011).

It is important to note that learning intentions should relate to what students will learn (as opposed to what they will do). They should articulate, in student-friendly language, what is going to be taught in a lesson. They should also be decontextualized, particularly if the context is not a key element to the skill. For example, suppose a lesson is focused on unpacking the unfamiliar language of *To Kill a Mockingbird*. In that case, it might be more appropriate for the learning intentions to focus on developing general strategies for making meaning of unfamiliar language instead of focusing on the language in the novel itself. This does not mean the novel is irrelevant; rather, it makes the intended learning more explicit and increases the likelihood of the strategies being transferred.

To create learning intentions, it can help to reflect on what you want your students to learn. For example, are they going to be learning new knowledge? Develop or practice new skills? Or, instead, deepen their understanding? Table 12 provides some example learning intentions to helped get you started.

Table 12. Example Learning Intentions

Knowledge: • Know why rabbits are an ecological disaster in the wild. • Know how to construct a pie chart. • Know about different forms of energy. • Know what causes lightning.
Skills: • Be able to identify persuasive strategies used by the author or an argument. • Be able to work as part of a team. • Be able to solve a problem using more than one strategy. • Be able to write a recount.
Understanding: • Understand how the internet can be used for research purposes. • Understand the effects of diet on health. • Understand the causes of an historical event. • Understand what happens when the human body consumes carbohydrates.

To ensure that learning intentions are effective, they should be coupled with success criteria, which are the markers used to determine if learners have met the learning intentions and how well or to what standard they have been met. A great strategy that can support the use of learning intentions and success criteria is the use of worked examples to show students what success looks like, as this can help students to:
1. Understand the value of what they are learning.
2. More explicitly understand the purpose of their teacher's lessons.
3. Better use feedback as they are learning to move towards success.

Note: We will consider worked examples in greater detail later.

It is worth considering co-constructing the success criteria with your students. Such an activity might take time but can be a powerful opportunity to build your students' understanding of what it takes to succeed. One approach to co-constructing success criteria involves providing your students with the opportunity to compare and contrast examples of work, identifying their key features, and determining what is missing or wrong in a work sample. You could also share annotated worked examples at different levels of quality so that students understand how the quality of work progresses. Alternatively, you can provide several samples of work ranging in quality and ask students in groups to discuss the features of each piece of work, including strengths, weaknesses, and what evidence of proficiency they see being demonstrated in each piece of work. Their observations will form the basis for what success criteria for the task should be. If you are feeling particularly adventurous, you might extend this work and consider providing your students with an opportunity to co-construct the assessment rubric.

As an alternative to product or task-focused success criteria, it is worth considering success criteria focused on processes; that is what students need to do during the learning process. Doing so can help students by providing guidance on the steps required to progress toward the learning intention; see Table 13 for two great examples adapted from Clarke (2019).

Table 13. Product vs Process Success Criteria

Learning Intention: To be able to use the column method to multiply two-digit numbers by a single digit.		
Success Criteria (Product) By the end, you will have: • At least five correct answers • Used your times table facts • Lined up the columns.	VS	**Success Criteria (Process)** To be successful, you need to have: • Estimated the answer first • Multiply units column first and carry any tens • Multiplied the tens and added any carried number • Checked your answers.
Learning Intention: To be able to use effective adjectives.		
Success Criteria (Product) By the end, you will have: • You will have used at least five adjectives.	VS	**Success Criteria (Process)** To be successful, you need to have: • Used the adjectives before the noun • Used adjectives that add something that the reader doesn't know. • Helped the reader imagine what you are describing through their senses.

Note: Using process-focused success criteria does not de-privilege the content or context within which learning has happened or knowledge that is required. Still, it does highlight the importance of transferable learning.

Create Appropriate Challenge

Rigour, challenge, and high standards for our students are good. If we push them too far, though, or not enough even, we can risk setting back both their engagement and learning through either frustration or boredom. When thinking about optimal challenge, an often cited example is that of computer game development. Computer game developers construct their games knowing that people want to be challenged. Indeed, when gameplay is too simplistic or too easy, then players can become bored. When a game is experienced as sufficiently and appropriately challenging, though, and the challenge increases with the player's learning or proficiency, the player will feel in 'flow.' When in flow, a player finds the balance between challenge and ability in the activity, as well the balance of boredom and frustration that results in the experience of success and satisfaction (Csikszentmihalyi & Csikszentmihalyi, 1975; Csikszentmihalyi, 1997). In education, these ideas are about managing and massaging the balance between the Zone of Actual Development and Zone of Proximal Development (Vygotsky, 1978). That is what our students can do unaided and what they can do with and support. A nice way to integrate these two concepts is Basawapatna, Koh and Nickerson's (2013) concept of Zone of Proximal Flow. Figure 13 illustrates flow state as the interface between ZPD and ZAD.

Figure 13. Finding Flow

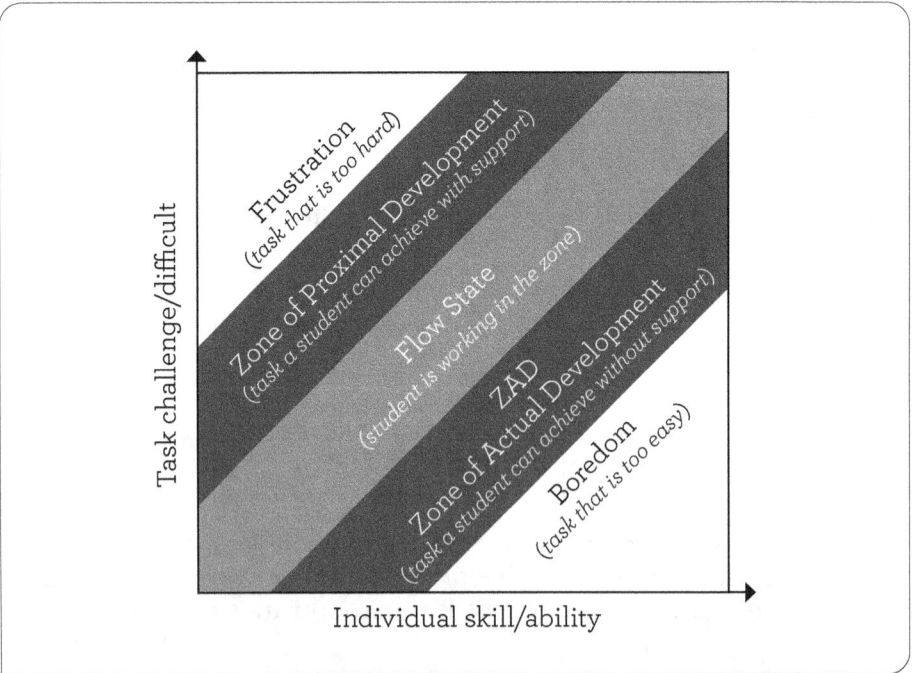

Our objective as teachers is not to set an unreasonably difficult target for our students. Instead, it is to encourage them towards an appropriately high standard that is achievable. The intention being that, like in gaming, it might be a target that they fail at some of the time, but the difficulty is not be so far beyond their reach that they give up, the result being that, through persistence, they will be rewarded with both success and the thrill of learning. As teachers, we need to target the Zone of Proximal Flow and just beyond. In thinking about computer games as the gold standard for finding this flow state, when playing computer games, students know what success looks like at the next level; it is not just doing for the sake of doing. This is an important reminder for us as to the potency of using learning intentions and success criteria.

Setting an appropriately challenging standard for our students can be difficult. If this is an area you are focused on improving, you need to use strategies for identifying or diagnosing the needs of your students as a part of your planning and instruction. This means using effective pre-assessment strategies to determine the current level of your students' knowledge, understanding, capability, and engagement in learning before you commence planning instruction. Capturing this data, you will inevitably discover a diverse range of instructional levels in your class. This might seem overwhelming at first, but it is entirely normal. In fact, it is important to accept that this is OK. What's not OK, though, is if you ignore this and plan lessons expecting ALL students to simultaneously work at the same level of challenge. This can be challenging to deal with but armed with good pre-assessment data, you will be better equipped to target learning for all students to ensure that they are appropriately challenged.

Build in Time for Review

Reviewing what has been learned is critical to ensuring that knowledge and skills are transferred from short-term to long-term memory. This is because, according to the trace decay theory of memory, a memory leaves a neurochemical mark or 'trace' in your brain, a bit like a path that is made by people walking through a forest – the more traffic along the same path, the more worn the pathway becomes. Likewise, if the same path is not used often, then it will eventually become overgrown. Further, trace decay theory proposes that whether or not information will be easily remembered is a result of the amount of time between a memory's formation and recall. The implication is that shorter intervals of time will support greater recall, whereas longer periods will result in more information being forgotten. In the same way, learned facts can be forgotten when not reviewed. In fact, a recent study has shown that information captured in short-term memory will only last a few seconds if it is not rehearsed (McKeown et al., 2019).

A well-known study on forgetting by Spitzer (1939) compared the percentage of remembered material from a textbook at different intervals of time after exposure. His results are illustrated in Figure 14.

Figure 14. Decrease of Recall Over Time

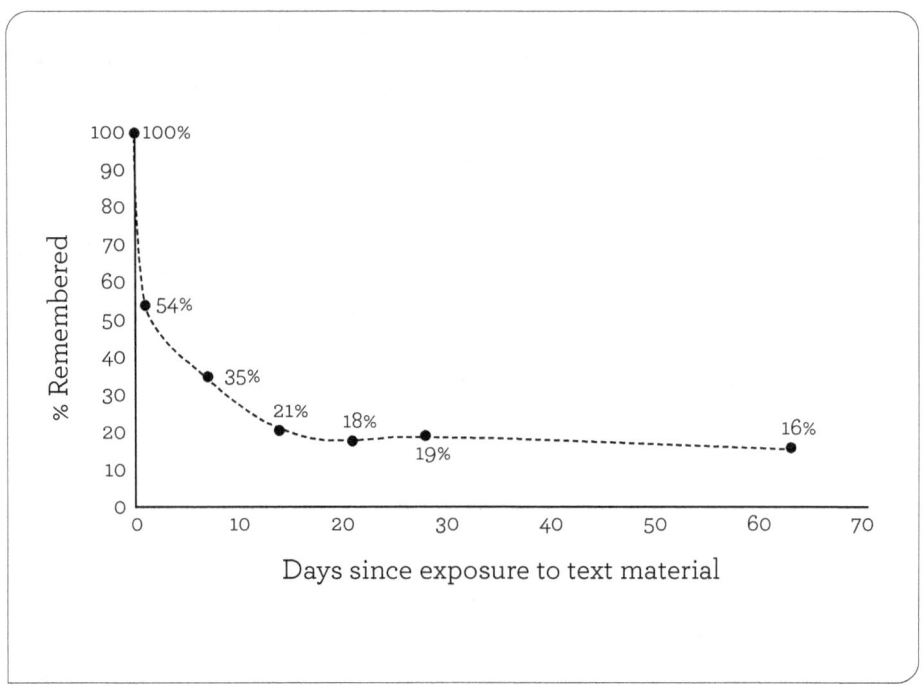

Spitzer's results illustrate nicely the forgetting curve, which Hermann Ebbinghaus first hypothesized in the 19th century. A key takeaway is that most learned information will be lost from memory relatively quickly. Fortunately, a secondary takeaway is that with regular review, this can be overcome. Indeed, as part of his studies on forgetting, Ebbinghaus described another concept called 'overlearning'. The basis of overlearning is that if you practice something more than is necessary to memorise it, then it is overlearned, and the information is stored more strongly.

Ultimately, this means that as teachers, it is our responsibility to ensure that we take time to pause and review with our students what has been learned. The best time to review is within a day or two of the material being read or learned. This means it makes sense to review not only what has been learned during a lesson but also from the last few lessons.

As a final comment, maybe something we need to recognise is that perhaps we are not as good at teaching the skills of consolidating understanding as we need to be and that we should take time to support our students to developed these skills so that they can actively participate in their learning. What an excellent opportunity to also help our students understand how to recognize their learning and celebrate their progress and improvement; doing this can go a long way to enhance their sense of self-efficacy through the experience of mastery.

EXPLANATION

Clarity through explanation is more than simply whether a teacher's diction is clear. Rather, it relates to whether a teacher's instruction is understandable to their students. Essentially, this is about a teacher being able to explain new content to students clearly. To do this, the teacher must introduce new content in small, engaging steps while at the same time relating it to past learnings. They must repeat and stress directions and draw students' attention to common mistakes and areas of difficulty.

If enhancing clarity through explanation is something that you have decided to focus on improving in your classroom, then there are several principles to consider.

Principles for Clarity of Explanation

- Teach, check, repeat.
- Listen, respond.
- Build language to build knowledge.
- Understand your students and add to your toolkit.

The following sections draw upon these principles to overview some simple strategies to help you nurture clarity through explanation in your classroom.

Teach, Check, Repeat

If the goal of teaching is about enhancing student learning, then this is more about responding to our students' needs than delivering a curriculum. This means we need to learn how to be responsive to our students. In later sections, we learn about strategies to check for understanding (see page 102) and connecting the new knowledge with the old insights (see pages 104–105), both of which can be useful for gaining insights to meet the needs of students better. Beyond the use of 'hard' assessment data, this section is about using responsive formative strategies to engage our students in their learning, understand how they are coping with it, and respond as needed to address student misconceptions. Key to this is having strong pedagogical content knowledge, as discussed earlier.

Fundamental to this is that as we teach, it is necessary to confirm that our explanations and examples are understood and make sense to our students. This does not mean waiting until the test at the end of the week or unit of work. It means that once you have finished explaining a critical point, theory, process, or answered a question, it is important to ask clarifying questions to ensure that our students understand. It is unacceptable to ask a simple question and look up to see if students nod or give a thumbs up before moving on. Rather, it is necessary to ask a question, collect 'evidence', and respond accordingly. To do this, you might ask a question and have students provide an answer using a mini whiteboard. Alternatively, other technology-driven options can make data collection very efficient. Examples include Plickers, Padlet, Socrative, Quizzizz, and Kahootz, to name but a few. How your students respond will give you insights into their understanding and help you make any decisions about where to progress next with the lesson. For example, your class might be ready to progress, or they might need you to review certain key concepts, or there might be several students that require individual follow-up while the rest of the class continues.

When planning your questions, be careful. This is because the type of question you ask can impact the quality of information you collect. For example, asking closed questions, which generally call for simple yes/no responses, will tell you if students were able to answer a question, but they will not tell you why this is the case. On the other hand, open-ended questions allow students to provide more detailed information; this will yield much greater insight into student thinking and understanding. Neither approach is wrong per se – it is just important to consider what interpretations about your students and their learning you wish to make. No matter which you choose, taking time to ask authentic questions shows your students that you are interested in them and concerned that they understand; this goes a long way to building your classroom's vibe.

Listen, Respond

It is crucial to make sure that we listen to our students' needs in class and respond to their questions. It can, of course, be easy to become frustrated when students ask lots of questions. Please try to resist that reaction, though, because as previously discussed, our students can tell if we are interested in them and their learning, and showing frustration can do a lot of damage to the relationships we are trying to foster. A better approach is to presume positive intent in our students and be happy that they are engaged enough in the class and their learning to ask questions. I have always tried to make it clear to students that I am very thankful for their questions and make it clear they are demonstrating leadership and providing me with the opportunity to grow by thinking about how to meet their needs better. When listening, it is important to paraphrase or summarise a question before answering, as this can help minimise misunderstanding. This is especially important when in a group setting. Also, repeating a question for the entire class to hear can help everyone learn from a student's question. Listening and responding is not necessarily limited to what happens in the classroom, nor is it simply about when you are standing at the front of the class talking to your class. It might be responding to what you hear or see as you move around a classroom, looking over a student's shoulders as they work on a problem. It might be responding to an email from a student or engaging in a conversation. It might even be connecting with a student following a discussion with a parent. No matter the source, responding to our students shows them we care.

Build Language to Build Knowledge

Every subject has its own unique 'language' or 'literacy'. For example, mathematics uses words like 'equation' or 'coefficient'. Science has words like 'kinetic energy' and 'gravity'. Even literature has its vocabulary with words like 'alliteration' and 'allegory'. Such language can be pretty esoteric and confronting. As such, students can potentially struggle to understand subject-specific language, impacting their capacity to succeed. Therefore, we as teachers must commit time to teach the vocabulary and literacy of our subject areas.

If this is an area of focus for you, then strategies to help your students understand the foreign language in your subject include:

Scaffold the beginning
When introducing new vocabulary, first provide a description of the words. Then, ask students to create a description using their own words. It might be helpful to suggest to your students to use pictures or diagrams as memory cues to help them remember in the future.

Use everyday language
When introducing vocabulary or concepts, explain them using more accessible terms or everyday language. For example, the mathematical term 'variable' might be described as 'a letter which stands for an unknown or missing number'.

Build on Prior Knowledge
Prior knowledge can help link a new word to a concept your students have already learned. For example, suppose your class has been learning about how water molecules speed up and spread out during the process of evaporation. In that case, you could explain how condensation is the opposite process that causes them to slow down and move closer together.

Relevant or Related Words
It can be helpful to use a related or similar word when introducing new vocabulary. For example, the word 'judicial' can be linked to 'judge', as students usually know what a judge is. Or, in mathematics, the words numerator and denominator are often mixed. A great way to help students remember is to link the 'd' in the word denominator to the word 'down', which is linked to its position.

Regular Exposure
It is important to ensure that your students engage with the specific language and vocabulary of your subject regularly. This can help to consolidate new knowledge. Opportunities to do this can arise through discussion, word games, or annotated glossaries.

Use Imagery
Having students draw a picture or create a visualization is a powerful way to support learning. Indeed, research has found that drawing information is a powerful strategy to boost memory (Fernandes, Wammes & Meade, 2018).

Understand Your Students and Add to Your Toolkit

No matter where you teach in the world, the students who enter our classrooms have diverse life experiences and interests. It is therefore important that we as teachers do two things.

Firstly, we need to understand a bit about our students' life experiences and interests and use this information to inform our instruction and plan activities with which they will feel connected and engaged. For example, not all students may be interested in or know a particular sport, so it might be unwise to use examples that draw upon this sport without providing better context. Or you might have many international students in your class, which means that using resources that are dense in complex English language might be a poor choice. To understand our students, it can be helpful to run a class survey at the beginning of the year or semester asking students about their strengths and weaknesses and their topics of interest with regards to your subject.

Secondly, as teachers, we need to develop a broad range of strategies to have at our disposal to draw upon when interacting with students. For example, as a mathematics teacher, I have had to use a variety of approaches to support students' learning to solve equations. My choice was dependent on the developmental readiness of the student I was helping. Further, the students in our classes also have a variety of learning preferences. As such, having a diverse set of learning tasks and explanations spanning a range of modes can be helpful to ensure that all your students have multiple opportunities to engage with new knowledge and strategies.

Now, I want to make a point here lest I be accused of peddling the outdated 'Learning Styles' neuromyth. I do not subscribe to the proposition that people learn better when a lesson is presented in their preferred learning style. The fact is that the research is in, and learning styles have well and truly been debunked (for example, see Pashler et al., 2008). That said, I believe that for teachers, it is important to be mindful that our students do have a range of preferences for learning, and it can be helpful to target a diverse range of them as we plan and implement our teaching. This is for several reasons. Firstly, using a variety of learning modalities will enhance both student interested and engagement in your lessons. And, secondly, it will challenge your students to think in various ways, some of which might make them uncomfortable.

EXAMPLES AND GUIDED PRACTICE

Clarity through examples and guided practice is about how effectively a teacher demonstrates the relevant skills and processes that students are expected to be able to do and, of equal importance, give students practice tasks focused on what they need to know and be able to do. As a part of this, a teacher must provide examples of answers and solutions to post-test or summative assessment-type questions that students are likely to be assessed with to make the success criteria for learning obvious. Teachers must provide enough time, support, and guidance to students to practice and consolidate their learning (i.e., answering questions, providing appropriate feedback).

If improving clarity in your classroom through examples and guided practice is a priority for you, then there are several important principles for you to consider.

Principles for Clarity Guided Practice and Examples

- Illuminate the path.
- Show them what to do with examples.
- Highlight your thinking.
- Provide opportunities for practice.
- Encourage mastery.
- Build self-monitoring learners.

The following sections draw upon these principles to overview some simple strategies to help you nurture clarity through examples and guided practice in your classroom.

Illuminate the Path

As teachers, it is essential to ensure that we are transparent about what our students need to do to achieve success. As I have said previously, achieving success should not be a guessing game for our students. At the very base, this means that at the beginning of a subject, course, or year, we must hand out a syllabus that explicitly defines what is expected of them to achieve success. In addition, each lesson should include an explanation of the objective for what students are learning. Each of the above is about mapping out learning intentions and success criteria (see page 83 for a more detailed overview). On top of explicit learning intentions and success criteria, it can also be worthwhile showing students a spectrum of work samples. This is so they appreciate the difference between high- and low-quality work and become more adept at assessing their progress. It can also be helpful to use quality rubrics which will be discussed later (see the *Assessment of Student Learning* section starting on page 100).

In addition to showing your students what success looks like, the following suggestions go a long way to supporting them build their capacity to think about their thinking and what is required to be an effective leaner – aka metacognition.

Organisation is Key
Help your students be better organised by encouraging the use of a daily planner and structured folders and using a clean area set aside for dedicated study.

Help-seeking
Explain to your students the importance of being open with emotions and struggles. Remind them that if they are struggling, they should reach out and seek help from you, other teachers, peers, parents, or mentors.

Focus on Growth
Talk to your students about the value of developing a growth mindset. Remind them mistakes are beneficial and can teach us important lessons. Talk to your students about the importance of not comparing themselves with others and focusing their energy on their own journey and growth by focusing on personal improvement goals over absolute achievement goals. Although I would argue that if you focus on improvement goals, you will ultimately succeed with achievement goals.

Work Ethic
Encourage your students to translate their work ethic and determination into their studies from other aspects of their lives. For example, it can be powerful for a student to understand that dedication and responsibility demonstrated through a part-time job or sporting activity can actually be transferred into how they approach their education.

Perspective
Help your students visualize the big picture by talking with them about why school is important and how it can help open future opportunities. This is about assisting them to see the link between what they are learning and the pathways it might open later in life.

Diligence
Encourage your students not to procrastinate. Talk to them about the value of cultivating good habits such as finishing homework straight after school, regularly reviewing and revising their work, and seeking assistance when needed and how these can help shape a successful future. As Confucius once said, the expectations of life depend upon diligence; the mechanic that would perfect his work must first sharpen his tools.

Questions
Students should be encouraged to understand that there are no stupid questions and that asking questions and being curious is a necessary part of learning.

Show Them What to Do With Examples

A worked example is an explicit, detailed explanation of how to complete a task (Clark, Nguyen & Sweller, 2006). The worked-example effect is predicted by cognitive load theory and relates to the improved learning seen when worked-examples are integrated into instruction (Sweller, 1988). Using worked examples as an instructional strategy is perhaps one of the earliest and probably the best-known cognitive load reducing techniques (Pass, Renkl & Sweller, 2003). They have been shown to reduce cognitive load during the skill acquisition and as a result, enhance student learning. Further, research has shown that using worked examples effectively supports the development of complex problem-solving skills (van Merriënboer, 1997).

What this means is that a teacher can use worked examples to show students what success looks like, explicitly model for students the steps needed to complete a problem, and scaffold student knowledge and skill acquisition by using a series of examples. The intention of this is to help their students progress from learning by following a worked example as a reference point to solving problems on their own. When doing this, each new worked example needs to be appropriately challenging for the learner. It should be noted that the use of worked examples is not effective for all learners as they can lose their effectiveness for learners with greater levels of proficiency (Renkl, 2005).

Highlight Your Thinking

How do your students know what you expect of them and how to achieve what you ask of them?

To help our students understand what is expected of them, we can provide them with clear examples of how to use a skill/strategy and what is required to achieve success through explicit modelling. Teachers can provide such guidance to students by:
- Clearly articulating the features of a strategy or the steps required to perform the skill or use the strategy being learned.
- Breaking a skill into small parts, which can also help to decrease the cognitive load.
- Modelling different ways to tackle a problem.
- Giving them a problem with working that leads to the wrong answer and ask them to work out why the answer is wrong and what strategies and knowledge are needed to get it right.

Be transparent – think aloud!

A great strategy to help your students see your thinking is called, quite appropriately, Think Aloud. Personally, I have found the Think Aloud method to be a really helpful approach to surface my thinking for students – it is an approach I have used many times throughout both my career and my academic research. The power of this method is that it exposes to your students the internal processes that you use to engage in completing a task or solving a problem. This can help students understand what they need to do to be successful and help them learn to monitor their thinking and learning.

To use the Think Aloud method as a part of your teaching practice, you need to explicitly share what you are thinking while engaging in a task. This means pausing to verbalise:
1. What you see when looking at a task problem.
2. The questions you are asking yourself as you make sense of the problem and what you need to do.
3. Your decision about the tools and strategies to use to complete the task.
4. The steps you take and what you think while completing the task and checking your solution against the question.

As an example, if you are a mathematics teacher, you might use Think Aloud to model the solution to a question. Below, I have included an example internal dialog as I solve a problem for your reference.

1. **Solve for 'x' in the above diagram**

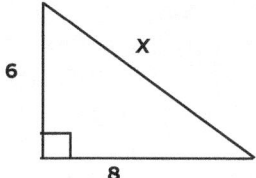

What I see here is a right-angled triangle. The first thing that leaps to mind is that this means I am going to need to use Pythagoras' theorem, which is $c^2=a^2+b^2$. What I notice is 'x' is the hypotenuse; this means that x^2 will be equal to 6^2 plus 8^2. 6^2 is equal to 36 and 8^2 squared is 64 so 36 + 64 = 100, this means $6^2 + 8^2 = 100$ so the answer is 100. Let's check. Ahh, no that is what x^2 is. I need to take the square root of 100, which is 10. This means 'x' is equal to 10. Okay, one last check, are there any units in this question? Nope. The answer is 'x' = 10 units.

Using Think Aloud is not limited to mathematics. Here are some other examples:
- A humanities teacher might use the method to model how they put together an essay plan.
- A science teacher could use the approach to discuss the scientific process or experiments.
- An English teacher might use Think Aloud while reading a text to model the types of questions they use to make sense of the text.
- A health and physical education teacher might use the strategy to describe in detail how they are performing a skill whilst playing a game.

The possibilities are endless, really; the key is making sure that you explicitly share what you are thinking while engaging in a task or activity.

If you are interested in using Think Aloud as a strategy, then the following steps adapted from resources create by The Texas Education Agency (nd) might be helpful.

Step 1. Setting-up for success

If Think Aloud is new to you or you like to be completely prepared, it can be important to take some time to plan. This means choosing the activity you would like to model. As you prepare, make sure you try to see the task through the eyes of your students. This means thinking about what they need to know how to do. It can be helpful at this point to draw upon your experiences of content, skill, or strategy and consider what needs to be made explicit for your students. As you prepare, you might also find it helpful to do a dry run before the class. This can help you decide where you might like to stop and think aloud and plan what you would like to say. To help with this, you might like to annotate a copy of the task, writing down questions, comments, and your thoughts as you go; if you do this, you are creating a great resource that you can share with your students to help consolidate their understanding of your thinking.

Note: In contrast to the above, I have found, as I have gained experience, that I am comfortable tackling problems sight unseen. For me, this feels more authentic, and my students get to see me genuinely grapple with a problem, working through my toolkit to find a solution. They also get to see the joy I experience when I am successful.

Step 2. Thinking Aloud

When using Think Aloud with your class, you should explain to them what the process is, what it involves, and why it is a helpful method to support their learning. It is important that your students know that the purpose of this method is for them to be able to observe you as you think, not to interact with you. Let them know that they will have a chance to ask questions and make comments when you debrief afterward.

Once your students are ready, you can begin your Think Aloud. Start by displaying the activity or problem prompt. Make sure there is a copy available for students (either paper or digital) so that they can copy your steps and make annotations as needed.

Next, you can begin by thinking aloud as you engage with the activity. As you do, make sure that you progress slowly enough so that your students can follow along and that you are pausing as you had intended. It can also be helpful to underline, highlight, or circle any keywords or parts of the problem prompt that trigger a thought or the use of a skill or strategy.

Step 3. Debriefing the learning

Once you have completed your Think Aloud activity, it is a good time to debrief with your students. This is an opportunity to ask students to share what they saw. To identify what they saw you do to complete the activity, including the steps you followed, the strategies that you used, what worked, what didn't work, and anything they were confused about – this can form the prompt for the next steps in the lesson. This is also a powerful opportunity to ask your students how the strategies they saw you use might transfer to complete other problems or activities.

Beyond using Think Aloud to model your thinking, you can encourage your students to use the Think Aloud method when they are solving problems, particularly those that are challenging. This is because it can help students to become much better at monitoring and regulating their own learning.

Provide Opportunities for Practice

We all know that if you want to get better at something that practice is paramount. The key to this is that practice is necessary for skills to become internalised and build automaticity. To build expertise, then, our students must practice the skills and strategies they are learning. It is important then for us as teachers to provide opportunities for our students not just to practice but to practice correctly. This is entirely in line with the comment attributed to the American Football coach Vince Lombardi:

Practice does not make perfect.
Only perfect practice makes perfect.

Lombardi's sentiment is supported by Tony Buzan, British psychologist and author of several books about memorising and effectiveness, who has pointed out that practice only helps people to repeat what they are already doing. It doesn't necessarily help them perfect it. The thing is, practice is only great if what is being practiced is being done right.

So, what is perfect practice? And what does it mean for teachers?

Perhaps the best characterisation of 'perfect practice' is deliberate practice that necessitates a purposeful, intentional approach to improvement.

Deliberate practice involves several key elements:
1. It has the specific goal of improving performance.
2. It must be repeated. A lot.
3. Continuous feedback is a necessary ingredient.
4. It is more than likely very demanding and not much fun.

With deliberate practice and effective feedback, students can learn to self-regulate to master a new skill or concept. As teachers, our responsibility is to create opportunities for our students to practice what they are learning and to support them with targeted feedback.

A great approach to scaffolding deliberate practice into your classrooms is the strategy known as gradual release of responsibility. This approach is encapsulated by the phrase 'I do, we do, you do' and has the premise that a new skill's learning and cognitive load should be shifted slowly from teacher to student. This is achieved through modelling, supported practice, and individual practice; the time over which this occurs will depend on the skill/concept being learned. To capture the power of collaborative and cooperative learning, this model can be modified as:

*I do, we do, you do together,
you do independently.*

I do

The process of gradually releasing responsibility starts with you modelling to students what to do. At this stage, you need to be explicit about how to use the skill being taught and the steps that need to be followed. This is a great time to provide scaffolding, taking time to talk through tasks step-by-step. During this phase, it is good to keep students actively engaged in the lesson; for example, ask them to copy down notes or vocabulary, write a summary, describe the process, or make and explain predictions or their ideas. As discussed in the previous section, Think Aloud is a great strategy to share how you engage with a task.

We do

This step is about guided practice, or what Professor Barbara Rogoff called guided participation. Here you look to create opportunities to work with your students in completing a task. To start with, you might purposefully choose one or two students, who you know understand what is being learned, to help solve a problem. These students will act as role models to the rest of the class and help others see that success. Alternatively, you could choose someone you know has a common misconception to help surface an issue that needs to be addressed. The next step might be to call on one or two students randomly (doing so can help holds all students to account and keep them focused – strategies for being random were discussed earlier in the book). Finally, open up for volunteers. This process aims to offer an alternative to what is seen in many classrooms, where teachers call on volunteers first. A quick note, the students who share ideas during this phase, should not be the only students engaged. Again, students should be involved during this phase; this might include calling out or suggesting ideas or steps.

You do together

This step does not appear in the original descriptions of the 'I do, We do, You do' approach, but I love it as it is an excellent opportunity to use the high-impact strategies of cooperation and collaboration to enhance student participation learning. In this step, students should work in groups to practice what is being learned. Examples of strategies include having students seated and working together in pairs, triads, or small groups. It can also be helpful to ensure all students have a specific role to ensure each of them are on task and have equal involvement within their group. Throughout this phase, you should move around the classroom to monitor student engagement and assist if needed. This can be a good opportunity to decide if individual students or the entire class needs additional support. It is also a great time to support smaller groups of students that need additional modelling or instruction.

You do (Independent practice)
This is the final phase, and it involves allowing our students to practice and apply their skills and knowledge independently. This phase is, or should be, the ultimate purpose of our work – to help our students reach the point where they can apply the skills they have learned independently.

Encourage Mastery

Ensuring students develop mastery is arguably one of the overarching goals for teachers. For a student to have achieved mastery means that information is not simply memorised for a test but is learned at the level of deep conceptual understanding in line with the stated learning intention and success criteria for the topic or course. Mastery learning is an educational philosophy and an instructional strategy that Benjamin Bloom first proposed in 1968. The basis of mastery learning is that students need to demonstrate mastery of a topic before moving forward in their learning. If a student has not yet demonstrated mastery, they must be given further support until mastery is reached and they are ready to move on. A key feature of mastery learning is that different students can require different amounts of time and opportunity to engage with the same material to achieve equivalent mastery. This is in complete contrast to more traditional approaches to teaching in which all students are taught the same curriculum over the same time frame. Mastery learning, therefore, shifts responsibilities in the classroom so that a student's failure to achieve mastery is not necessarily due to a lack of ability on their part but rather the instruction and time allowed for learning. In mastery learning, then, the big challenge for educators is using appropriate instructional strategies and planning effective use of time to ensure all students can achieve to the same level (Bloom, 1981).

Mastery learning is perhaps one of the most well-known and widely researched teaching methods. While challenging to implement, when embedded well, mastery learning approaches are highly successful. For example, in a meta-analysis of 46 studies, Guskey and Pigott (1988) found consistently positive effects across several variables, including achievement, retention of learned material, engagement, and student affect. In support of this, Kulik, Kulik, and Bangert-Drowns (1990) investigated 108 studies of mastery learning programs finding positive effects in favour of the teaching strategies. Further, Hattie's visible learning research has synthesized 14 meta-analyses and found mastery learning approaches have an overall effect size of 0.61.

If integrating mastery learning into your approach to teaching and learning is an area of focus, you need to use strategies to identify the needs of your students to inform your planning and instruction. This means using effective pre-assessment strategies (formal and informal) to determine the current level of your students' ability and engagement in learning before you commence planning the instruction for a lesson or unit of work. This is to ensure that you are considering what your students already know, can say, and do. Seeking such knowledge, you will inevitably discover that there are students at different instructional levels in your class. As discussed previously, this might seem overwhelming, but it is okay and actually normal. While some of your students might be ready for solving quadratic equations, others might still be struggling with linear equations. It is important to acknowledge that this is acceptable. What is not acceptable is if we expect all students to be working on the same material simultaneously. This can be challenging but armed with good pre-assessment data, you will be better equipped to target learning for all students to ensure that they are appropriately challenged.

ASSESSMENT OF STUDENT LEARNING

The reality is that a teacher can't communicate effectively with their students without regularly seeking and responding to feedback from them (Fendick, 1990). Within the classroom, this means that we must actively pursue and respond to a diverse range of feedback types from and about students. This is about making sure that we as teachers clearly understand how our students are engaging with and progressing with new learning and responding accordingly. We can do this by utilising appropriate formative or responsive teaching strategies and assessment tools to evaluate student achievement, student progress, and our impact. This marks the distinction between formative and summative evaluation of practice. Clarity through assessment of student learning also requires that we are transparent with our students about the purpose and process of assessment.

If enhancing teacher clarity through assessment is something that you have decided to focus on improving in your classroom, there are several principles to consider.

Principles for Clarity of Assessment of Student Learning

- Highlight how assessment will occur.
- Check for understanding.
- Connect the new with the old.
- Provide formative feedback.

The following sections draw upon these principles to overview some simple strategies to help you nurture clarity through assessment of student learning in your classroom.

Highlight How Assessment Will Occur

As discussed previously, success criteria are the markers we use to determine whether and how well learners have met the intended learning intentions. Success criteria are a crucial ingredient, as they let our students in on the mystery of what it takes to demonstrate success. That is, they provide students with:
1. A roadmap against which to compare their work; and
2. An understanding of how they will be assessed.

The basic premise of success criteria is that if students have the same idea as their teacher regarding what is going on in the classroom, what they should be learning, and what success looks like, they are more likely to succeed. The power of providing such information to students cannot be understated. For example, after examining 31 meta-analyses, Hattie and Donoghue (2016) found an overall effect size of 0.54, indicating that the provision of success criteria to students is an above average influence on student learning.

An important approach to ensuring that students understand how they will be assessed are assessment rubrics. A rubric, usually in matrix form, is a scoring tool used to understand students' work against underlying criteria or curriculum standards. A good rubric is used to make explicit assessment criteria and expected performance standards for both students and teachers. Essentially, they help to show what is important and, if well-designed, highlight increasing levels of proficiency that students can demonstrate. Rubrics are not simply for academic subjects and can be designed for any cognitive, affective, or skills-based domain. For example, I have developed and used rubrics relating to mathematics, problem-solving, critical and creative thinking, and approaches to learning to name but a few.

There are many ways to design or create rubrics, but my preferred approach draws upon the work of Emeritus Professor Griffin from the

Assessment Research Centre at the University of Melbourne's Graduate School of Education. Patrick and his team have advocated an approach to writing rubrics by which a domain to be assessed broken up into strands, capabilities, and indicators. Each indicator is then articulated as a series of quality criteria that describe an increasing level of observable quality. The result of the process is a matrix of assessment rubrics that can be used to assess student attainment, inform instruction, and track student growth. See Patrick's book *Assessment for Teaching* for a much more detailed explanation.

A final consideration for using rubrics is that they can be a great way to inform discussions with students about their achievement on an assessment task and also support peer and self-assessment.

Check for Understanding

Checking for understanding is an essential step in the process of teaching and learning. Indeed, to be successful as a teacher, we need to check our students' understanding of what we have taught as it can help us to identify what to do next with our teaching. Further, if we do not check for understanding, it can be challenging to know precisely what the impact of our lessons, our teaching, is upon our students' learning. Finally, checks for understanding or formative assessment strategies that are used to inform teaching and feedback can also be a great way to track student learning throughout the process of instruction.

Checking for understanding through formative assessment strategies can help to ensure the success of all students by:
1. Providing teachers with a base from which to adapt planned instruction.
2. Giving students evidence of their progress to help them self-regulate their learning. This can also help students to track their progress.
3. Allowing us as teachers to provide ongoing feedback to our students. This can enable our students to feel supported in their learning and also to develop self-assessment and regulation strategies.

When formatively assessing, it is important to note that there is typically no final or summative grade assigned. This is because using grades effectively contradicts what formative assessments are for, that is, helping teachers *form* a belief upon which to act about what needs to happen next and supporting students to understand what they need to do next to improve. Further, the use of grades for assessing formatively, and assessing more generally, can be counterproductive and negatively impact learning, particularly when students take their grades personally. Rather, the purpose of using formative assessment strategies is to provide practice and feedback opportunities for our students as well as create a lens for ourselves into their current level of understanding and the impact of our teaching.

Formative assessment is then about using assessment data to inform what happens next. I would argue that the key to effective formative assessment is not how the data is collected nor the assessment tools used. Instead, it is about how we as teachers use the information gained, how it is interpreted and used to adjust our teaching. For example, more formal assessments, such as tests, which are typically used for grading purposes, can be used effectively for formative purposes when collected at the start of a unit of work and properly analysed. On the other hand, one of the primary benefits of formative assessment strategies is that they can be undertaken more informally during class time to gain moment-by-moment insights into how students are coping with the demands of the lesson.

There are so many great opportunities to make formative assessments about our students. For example, you might consider using exit tickets at the conclusion of a class, asking your students to respond to a prompt that focuses on the big ideas covered in the lesson. You could also ask them to write a brief reflection or draw a mind map summarising their learning. You can collect your students' responses as they leave the classroom and analysed them to help you check for your students' understanding of a concept taught. This can help you to determine how well your students have learned what has been taught and guide planning for your next class. During the class, you might try asking your students to use hand signals/gestures to indicate their understanding of content; I have found this very useful whilst running online sessions during remote learning school and university lockdowns during COVID-19. As an alternative, you might use mini whiteboards, asking students to respond to a question by writing on the whiteboard and turning it so the teacher can see.

The Think-Pair-Share strategies, outlined on Page 67-68, are excellent strategies by which you can gain real-time insights into your students' understanding of what they are learning. Another great approach is to give your students a checklist at the commencement of a class that outlines the success criteria for a task or lesson and asks them to self-assess. You can then collect the checklists and review them. You can also ask your students to write a sentence explaining how they know or why they think they are still struggling. Finally, taking time to observe our students during class should not be underestimated as a strategy for gaining moment-by-moment insights into student understanding. Watching our students' actions, behaviours and words as they work is a great strategy to gain valuable data and insights that can serve as a formative assessment allowing us to adjust our lessons as required.

If you plan to integrate checks for understanding or formative assessment into your planning and teaching practice, then some ideas to consider include:

- Ensure that you begin with the outcomes in mind. That is, understand what you want your students to know, say, make or do by the end of a lesson and make sure that you let them know through learning intentions and success criteria; don't keep it a secret!
- Plan for engaging lessons—combining targeted instruction, collaborative learning opportunities, guided instruction, and independent learning, all of which are aligned with your learning intentions and success criteria.
- Intentionally plan checks for understanding in your lessons from the outset – they should never be an add-on.

Finally, if you are integrating formative assessment strategies into your practice, you must be sure that you act based on the data you collect. This means the evidence you collect needs to inform what you do next. It must influence the instructional designs that you make. This is perhaps the most important idea as, in reality, formative assessment is not about collecting and having data. It is about what you do next to improve learning based on data.

Connect the New with the Old

> *The most important, single factor influencing learning is what the learner already knows. Ascertain this and teach them accordingly.*[7]
>
> (Ausubel, 1968, vi)

Constructivism is the educational theory that proposes that new knowledge is built upon existing knowledge. It is informed by the belief that we must support our students to connect what is being learned with their past experiences and learning. Thus, when planning, it is important to determine and critically consider what your students know and can do at the commencement of a lesson or unit of work. Unfortunately, though, teachers often spend considerable time on the busy work of gathering materials and resources to use during instruction without using the greatest resource at their disposal, their students. Most teachers are guilty of hurrying through to teach a concept or skill without slowing down to ask their students what they know about the topic. This may represent a wasted expenditure of time given that Graham Nuthall's (2007) work indicates that students typically already know 40%–50% of what is being taught in a class. A further challenge for teachers is that when we fail to bring forth our students' prior knowledge, we run the risk of seeing our students as vessels into which teachers must pour knowledge. This is what Freire (2006) referred to as the banking model of pedagogy.

There are a great many activities that we can use to gain insights into what our students know and support them to tap into their prior knowledge. For example, brainstorming is a classic strategy in which we show students a stimulus (an image, text, or video) or ask them a question about an upcoming unit of work and then ask them to outline everything they can about the topic. When brainstorming, you should make sure that you select a stimulus that will allow students to make the bridge to any new content, concepts, or skills your class will be learning. There are many ways to brainstorm. You might do so as a class or ask students to do so individually, in pairs, or in small groups and then feedback thinking to the class. A great option to scaffold brainstorming is Alphabet Brainstorming. To use this strategy, give students a sheet of paper with a box for each letter in the alphabet. Then ask students to work in pairs or small groups to brainstorm a word or phrase that is related to an upcoming topic that starts with each letter.

Another great strategy is the use of K-W-L charts, a type of graphical organiser designed to help students organise information before, during, or after a lesson. The letters KWL are an acronym for Know, Wonder, and Learned. The process of using K-W-L charts is relatively simple.

Firstly, have students respond to the first column prompt – What do I already know? They can do this individually or in groups and then report back. This is an excellent opportunity to understand what your students need to learn at the beginning of the lesson or unit of work. Next, have students respond to the column two prompt – What do I want to know? Answering this question can be difficult, particularly if it is a new topic, so you might want to scaffold by including the six key questions of journalism: Who? What? When? Where? Why? And, how? Column two creates a powerful opportunity for you to draw upon students' voices to plan your instruction. It also opens the door to introducing your hopes for their learning from the lessons or topics, including the learning intentions and success criteria.

Then through the lesson or unit of study, you can ask your students to reflect on the first two columns and add into the third column what they now know that they hadn't known earlier.

One final thought with regards to K-W-L Charts, at the conclusion of the lesson or series of lessons, you might like to consider asking your students to reflect on the strategies and processes they used when learning to identify the strategies they used and whether or not they were effective. What an excellent opportunity to help your students build their metacognitive skills and self-regulation.

Figure 15. Example K-W-L + S Chart

K-W-L+S Chart

Topic _____

K	What do I already know?	W	What do I want to know?	L	What have I learned?
S	How did I learn? What strategies work? What strategies don't work?				

Provide Formative Feedback

Feedback is one of the highest impact strategies that has emerged from Hattie's Visible Learning research. Being able to facilitate effective feedback as a teacher is then imperative. So, what exactly is good feedback then? Well, according to Hattie and Timperley (2007), feedback is information that is given by an agent, such as a teacher, about aspects of performance or understanding. It helps answer the questions: *Where am I going? How am I going? And, where to next?*

Essentially, effective feedback helps the receiver close the gap between where they are now and where they are going by telling them how to improve.

So, what is the problem? We all provide feedback, right?

Well, giving feedback does not imply that our students are receiving and acting upon it. Therefore, whilst a teacher may claim or believe that they are giving feedback, it is helpful to inquire into how well the feedback is received and subsequently acted upon by their students. The critical question for us as educators then is 'How do we give effective feedback to our students?'

The answer to this question is about:
1. Supporting your students to understand their current level of performance; and
2. Supporting them to understand what they need to do to improve.

Ideas for considering if feedback is an area of focus for you include:

Seek to provide affirmation
It is essential to let the students in our care know what they have done right as well as where they have made mistakes. Affirmative feedback is about telling your students that what they have done is correct. Affirmation should not be mistaken for praise, though, because personal praise (i.e., good boy or great job) focuses on the person instead of their work product or way of working.

Correction and redirection
Making mistakes is an important and necessary part of the learning process and a prerequisite for success. We all know students do not always do things correctly. What we might not have considered, though, is that when students make errors, it demonstrates that they feel safe enough to make mistakes and also that they are confident and willing enough to push beyond what they have already mastered. This is a good thing. Further, creating space for and allowing our students time to practice and make mistakes provides us with opportunities to put effective feedback strategies to good use.

When practising, it is important that our students recognise when they are struggling and need help to correct their mistakes. This is about helping them to develop their self-regulation. In such cases, our correction is not just letting them know they are incorrect. It is also necessary to point them in the right direction. That is, you need to correct and then redirect them. For many tasks, particularly simple tasks, this can be achieved by providing the answer or solution. For example, you might underline a misspelled word but also write the correct spelling next to it. As a further example, you could mark a question as wrong but also provide the right answer. For more complex tasks, this type of feedback might involve having a short meeting with your students and telling them what they could do to improve. Rubrics can be very useful in communicating expectations for an assignment and providing targeted feedback about their performance concerning established standards.

Make the process the focus of your feedback
While the correct and redirect approach to feedback can be effective, this is typically only for the work being commented on and is not necessarily transferable. If you focus on the processes being practised, you can support students improve on similar tasks. The intention of this is to show your students the link between their results, why they received the result, and what they must do to improve. For example, you can show your student the step(s) where they made a mistake in a task and then model the steps with a similar problem; if you do this, it is a good idea to give your students time to complete additional practice to ensure mastery. This type of feedback is not simply about the 'steps

in a process' though, but to help students connect their actions with the standard of their work. You can help students make this connection in many ways. For example, you might highlight the link between student achievement on a test and time spent studying or the relationship between results and the time spent on research or proofreading. Duckworth (2016) is another great example, having highlighted that grit, involving perseverance, passion, resilience, ambition, and self-control, is an important factor in achieving success.

Conferencing
One-on-one meetings with students can also be an effective strategy for providing feedback and allowing students dedicated time to ask questions. A good way to use conferencing is to meet with students one-on-one while the other students in your class are working independently. During a conference, have students write down notes as you are providing commentary. To facilitate this approach, consider staggering due dates for your students' assessment tasks. Doing so can help create the necessary time to provide quality, written feedback, and a rotation approach to conferencing.

Note, this idea of no having a fixed due date might be uncomfortable for some, but I encourage you to think more broadly about the purpose of assessment. From my perspective, the goal of most assessment tasks at school is really formative – to *inform* next steps. In which case, if a task is handed in today or tomorrow or next week is irrelevant if it means that the timeframe for feedback is reduced and students are then able to move on with their learning. As I progressed through my career, I became much happier pushing back on fixed due dates and more focused on adjusting what I did to meet my students' needs. I encourage you to do the same.

CHAPTER SUMMARY – BUILDING TEACHER CLARITY

The key message from this chapter is that teacher clarity is a powerful factor for teachers aiming to build their classrooms' vibe. Broadly speaking, the concept of teacher clarity is concerned with the beliefs that students have about the capability of a teacher to communicate effectively with them. More specifically, it is about student perceptions about their teachers' behaviours associated with organisation, explanation, the use of example, and guided practice and assessment to support student learning.

We have seen throughout this chapter many practical strategies that teachers can use to help build their *Teacher Clarity*.

REFLECTION QUESTIONS

Take some time to reflect on and answer each of these questions. Make notes or draw pictures.
 Do whatever helps you process the ideas and concepts discussed, and if you feel comfortable, share your answers with a colleague.

- How would you describe Teacher Clarity to a colleague?

- How can build your Teacher Clarity enhance your classroom vibe?

- What resonated for you in this chapter? What challenged you?

- How would you describe the status of your Teacher Clarity with your students? What evidence do you have to support this?

- Following this chapter, what ideas or strategies can you commit to trialing in your classroom this week?

- What sort of obstacles can you foresee stopping you?

- What strategies can you plan to overcome these obstacles?

CHAPTER 5

Considerations for Leaders

LEARNING INTENTIONS

In light of the lessons from this book, in this chapter, we will discuss implications for school leadership. In particular, we will discuss three crucial considerations to support school leaders think about how they might support teachers at their school to enhance their classroom vibe. By the conclusion of this chapter, you will:
- Understand three critical considerations for school leaders, including Self-Determination Theory, Collective Teacher Efficacy, and Teacher Agency, and how these might support your leadership.

I wrote this book firmly with teachers in mind. This was intentional. The key reason for this, as you might recall from earlier in the book, is that teachers have a significant impact on student learning, accounting for approximately 30% of the variation in student achievement, which is the largest influence beyond the variation attributable to students themselves.

Another way of considering this is that the impact of teachers accounts for 75% – 85% of the variation that falls *within* or is attributable to schools. In terms of the capacity for impact on student learning then, teachers are clearly important. Following, 15% – 25% of the within-school contributors to variation in student achievement are the school and school leadership. This is aligned to international research that tells us that the impact of school leaders is relatively moderate and primarily manifests itself indirectly through the organisational culture nurtured within the schools (Leithwood et al., 2004; Leithwood et al., 2019). Culture is the strategy – Drucker got it right again, it seems.

Figure 16. Influences on Student Learning (adapted from Hattie, 2003)

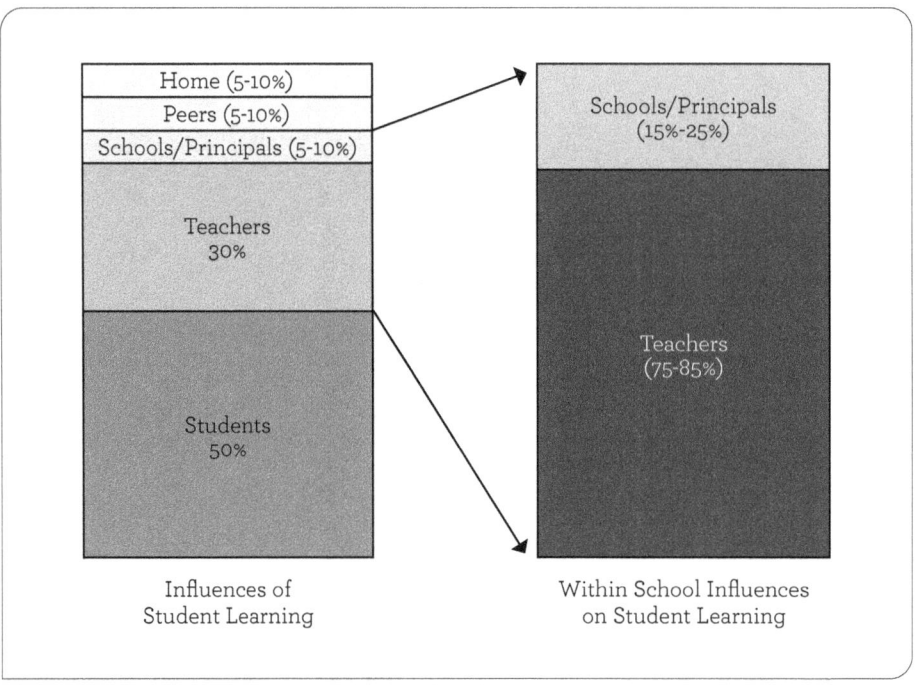

THE ROLE OF SCHOOL LEADERS

Given the context of what has been discussed in this book and the statistics that we have just seen, my argument is that school leaders have the key responsibility to harness the full potential impact of their teachers. To do this, I argue that school leaders must focus their efforts on building the culture within their school, the school vibe, if you will, such that their teachers are effectively empowered to understand and enhance the vibe in each of their classrooms. I argue that this should be one of the primary undertakings of school leadership. To achieve this, there are three key things that I believe are required of school leaders.

Primarily, they must accept that improving teaching practice is, as was discussed earlier, adaptive in nature. It is complex, hard to define, does not have a clear path to follow, and can take considerable time to achieve. What this means is that improving teacher practice is not about purchasing a program, sending someone to a professional development program, or bringing in an expert to talk about a given topic. Instead, it is much more about supporting those who need to enact the improvement, aka teachers, through the provision of space, time, and resources to engage in the hard work of change.

Secondly, and related to the previous point, and potentially difficult for leaders to swallow, while we know that the active participation of school leadership is essential for successful improvement, the more critical ingredient is the engagement and involvement of teachers. This means that no matter how alluring it might seem, a school leader cannot, and should not, see their role as about making decisions about the changes or initiatives that need to happen within their school. A leader should never see the school as an extension of themselves, an organisation over which they have dominion – I have experienced this, and it was a challenging experience. Indeed, as was discussed earlier, choosing strategies to implement is the easy part. As mentioned only a few moments ago, the real challenge is that implementing the adaptive change process required often necessitates the evaluation of personal and organisational values, beliefs, and behaviours combined with learning new collaborative ways of working together. Across my career, I have seen far too many high-potential initiatives suffer as leaders have ignored this exact point.

And, finally, given the above two points, school leaders must focus their work, their improvement efforts, on creating systems, structures, and processes to support and empower their teachers to make changes to improve their practice and enhance their classroom vibe. As a first step, this book has provided a framework that a single teacher or a team of teachers can use to evaluate and enhance their practice. To enhance classroom vibe at scale within a school, though, is a challenge. There are several ideas that I believe that school leaders must consider in seeking to meet this challenge. These ideas are captured within the interrelated concepts that sit behind Self Determination Theory, Collective Teacher Efficacy, and Teacher Agency – three critical concepts for leaders to understand.

Self-Determination Theory

Ryan and Deci's work on Self-Determination Theory (SDT) provides an important foundational lens through which school leaders should consider the implementation of change or improvement initiatives. SDT is a broad framework for considering psychological needs and human motivation, which evolved out of Ryan and Deci's work focused on motivation and goal-achieving behaviour (Deci & Ryan, 1985; Ryan & Deci, 2000). The research base of SDT has grown to include a diverse range of fields of human endeavour, including health, public safety, parenting, politics, religion and spirituality, and workplace leadership.

Central to SDT are the three base psychological needs of autonomy, competence, and relatedness. Autonomy is focused on an individual's experience of willingness and agency concerning one's behaviours. A comment I feel compelled to make is that autonomy does not necessarily mean having completely free will or unfettered independence over one's actions. Rather, it relates to individuals feeling a connection to and understanding of an organisation's goals combined with the freedom to pursue this goal, to feel agency, with a sense of control over how it is to be achieved. Competence relates to the need of individuals to feel successful and capable of doing good work. This is about experiencing ourselves as effective in what we do both in terms of the environment in which we are and the activities in which we are engaged. And relatedness is about feeling connected to others through close personal relationships. See Ryan and Deci (2017) for an overview of self-determination theory or <https://selfdeterminationtheory.org/>.

SDT proposes that when individuals are engaged in activities that meet their base psychological needs, they feel increasingly motivated. These types of activities are considered 'fun' or 'enjoyable' and when engaged in them, an individual is said to be driven by intrinsic motivation. Further, SDT proposes that when an individual's psychological needs are met, in addition to enhanced motivation and engagement, there is also enhanced well-being and performance.

Figure 17. Self Determination Theory

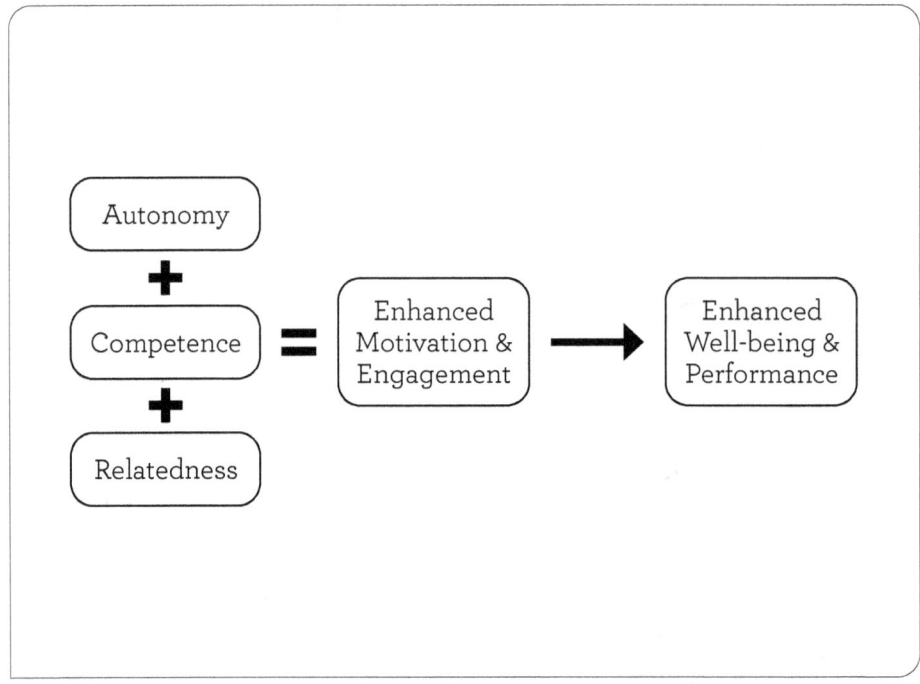

Further to the base psychological needs, motivation is a fundamental element of SDT. Rather than see motivations as a binary between intrinsic and extrinsic motivation where extrinsic motivation relates to an external source (i.e., a reward, a bonus, etc.) and in intrinsic motivation, the motivation is internal (i.e., for the sheer joy of it), SDT presents a more nuanced view of motivation with a graduated taxonomy or continuum of motivations through which an individual progress depending on how well their base needs are being met. This is illustrated in Figure 18 (Ryan & Deci, 2017).

Within this model, there are three categories of motivation: amotivation, extrinsic motivation, and intrinsic motivation.

1. Amotivation is when an individual demonstrates a lack of drive. They are not engaged and display a lack of interest, confidence, and agency.
2. Extrinsic Motivation is when an individual is driven by something external. It is broken into four discrete, incremental categories related to the source of the motivation progressing through external (driven by regards or punishment), introjected (driven by ego or desire for approval), identified (understanding importance of goal), and integrated (having alignment of goal with personal values).
3. Intrinsic Motivation is when the sole driver is being engaged in the task.

Figure 18. Continuum of Motivation[8]

Level of Self Determination	Low → High					
Motivation Form	Amotivation	Extrinsic				Intrinsic
How it is regulated	No-regulation	Externally	Introjection	Identification	Integration	Autonomously
Level of Needs Support	Low → High — Process of internalising based on presence of base psychological needs					
Drivers	No engagement, individuals lack confidence, sense of value, and agency.	Compliance based, driven by external demands, rewards, or punishments.	Based on approval from both oneself and others.	Based on an understanding of the utility and importance of the goal.	Based on the goal or activity aligning with personal values.	Engagement in the process for pure enjoyment.

Collective Teacher Efficacy

Another important consideration for school leaders is the concept of Collective Teacher Efficacy (CTE). The concept of CTE had its genesis in the seminal self-efficacy work of the late and great Albert Bandura. In particular, Bandura noted that when groups had shared or collective confidence in their ability to deliver on an outcome, this was associated with higher levels of success (Bandura, 1977). Bandura named this pattern Collective Efficacy. Through his work and the work of others, this phenomenon has been found to exist across many fields of human endeavour. These have included the workplace, sports teams, emergency services, communities, and of course, schools. Further, Bandura (1993) showed that when educators have confidence in their combined ability to impact student outcomes positively, then students' achievement is enhanced above and beyond the other influences students experience that might limit their capacity for success.

Figure 19. Enabling Conditions for Collective Teacher Efficacy

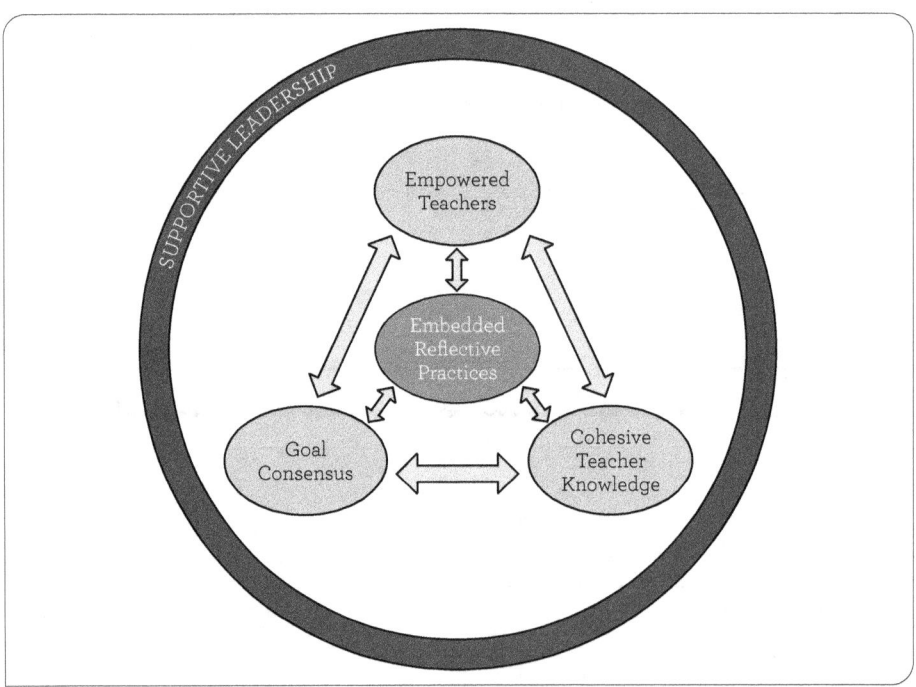

Collective Teacher Efficacy is a relatively nebulous term that relates to teachers' shared beliefs that they can positively influence student outcomes. Fortunately, through the work of Dr Jenni Donohoo, we now have a set of enabling conditions for collective teacher efficacy that have been summarised to support school leaders. These inter-related enabling conditions include Goal Consensus, Empowered Teachers, Cohesive Teacher Knowledge, Embedded Reflective Practice, and Supportive Leadership (Donohoo, 2017; Donohoo, O'Leary & Hattie, 2020; Hite & Donohoo, 2021).

Within the context of this Donhoo's framework, Goal Consensus relates to the nature of school-wide improvement goals, in particular, that they are understood by teachers. Empowered Teachers relates to the trust placed in teachers regarding their ideas and expertise and the engagement of teacher voice in decision making related to school improvement. Cohesive Teacher Knowledge relates to the nature of instruction and assessment practices and shared beliefs amongst teachers about the most impactful approaches combined with a capability to implement them effectively. It also integrates a shared awareness of the strategies used by teachers in the school. Embedded Reflective Practice relates to the presence of structures, protocols, and processes to support collaborative inquiry. The purpose of this is twofold. Firstly, to help teachers to draw upon feedback from both students and peers. And, secondly, to interrogate multiple sources of evidence when considering student progress and achievement. This is all to improve supporting teachers to examine and improve practice. And, finally, Supportive Leadership relates to how those in leadership roles engage with including showing authentic concern for the teachers, provide explicit support to teachers to complete their work effectively, and celebrating the success of individual teachers, teams, and the entire school community.

Teacher Agency

A final consideration for school leaders is that of teacher agency. Teacher Agency relates to the presence, or lack thereof, of a sense of autonomy or the empowerment of teachers within their school. There are various definitions of Teacher Agency but perhaps one of the most eloquent, thanks to school leader Barry Schon, is that it relates to a teacher's ability or perceived sense of ability to shape their work to progress through the challenges they encounter successfully. Focusing on Teacher Agency is important because it is almost the antithesis of often ineffectual top-down reform initiatives. Instead, it seeks to approach education from the bottom up by empowering teachers to take greater responsibility for the important work and decisions related to teaching and learning. Teacher Agency does not simply exist or manifest, though. It is cultivated through a teacher's disposition, self-efficacy, and the interplay of school-based conditions that support it. For example, the conditions associated with supporting Teacher Agency include structures that facilitate greater autonomy, a culture of psychological safety, teacher engagement in decision-making, teacher empowerment, and supportive leadership.

TYING IT ALL TOGETHER – IMPLICATIONS FOR SCHOOL LEADERS

This all sounds great, but what does this all have to do with me, you might ask?

From my perspective, two principles emerge across the ideas just considered that resonate for me and which I think are critical for school leaders to consider.

Firstly, I think school leaders must ensure that there is *clarity of direction* at their school. This means collaboratively crafting a comprehensive, compelling vision or purpose for their school. This is critically important, as it will provide teachers with a true north, a goal they can understand and hopefully align with their values. This is critically important for enhancing teacher autonomy because, as discussed before, autonomy is more about having a compelling goal one is connected to than having complete free will or unfettered independence over one's actions. An essential consideration for creating goal clarity is translating and unpacking the big picture school vision into what this means for teachers' day-to-day practice. This can help teachers understand how their work contributes to achieving the school's goals.

Related to this is the importance of clarifying how different initiatives that might emerge from a school's vision are related. This is because, in the busyness of school life, it can be difficult for teachers to see how the different tasks they are asked to perform are connected. The metaphor that I use for this is that school leaders need to highlight, to their staff, how the different threads (the initiatives) weave together to form the fabric or tapestry that makes up the school vision. A further consideration for ensuring clarity of direction is that it should be undertaken to invite and integrate teacher voice if it is practically possible.

Secondly, it is necessary to create structures to *support and empower* teachers to do the hard adaptive work of improvement. This is about recognising that once the direction is set, once the vision is clear, then for success to happen then, leaders need to get out of the way. This does not, of course, mean that leaders do not have a responsibility in all this. Of course, they do! They will still make decisions and guide direction. But in seeking to improve teaching and learning at their school, their job is to create and nurture supportive structures that allow teachers to do their work. This means embedding structures within the fabric of the school that bring teachers together to collaborate and reflect on their practice. This also requires putting into place training for leaders and protocols to support teachers in working together effectively. Doing so will enhance teacher autonomy, as teachers have the freedom to work together in pursuit of a school's goals. It will also build cohesive teacher knowledge, connectedness, and a collective sense of mastery as teachers come to learn from and with each other about how to be better teachers.

CHAPTER SUMMARY – CONSIDERATIONS FOR SCHOOL LEADERS

The key message from this chapter is that while school leaders are important in improving student learning outcomes, their real impact is through the teachers they lead. My argument is that school leaders have the responsibility to harness the potential impact of their teachers by focusing on building the culture within their school such that their teachers are effectively empowered to understand and enhance the vibe in each of their classrooms.

To do this, school leaders need to accept that improving teaching practice is, as was discussed earlier, adaptive in nature and create the space and time for teachers to engage in doing the hard work of change. This means that school leaders must focus their work, their improvement efforts on creating systems, structures, and processes to support and empower their teachers to make changes to improve their practice by focusing on their classroom vibe.

REFLECTION QUESTIONS

Take some time to reflect on and answer each of these questions. Make notes or draw pictures.
Do whatever helps you process the ideas and concepts discussed, and if you feel comfortable, share your answers with a colleague.

- Who makes the decisions about teaching and learning at my school?

- As a leader, how am I supporting and empowering my teachers to engage in the hard work of improving practice?

- How might our school's structures support or impede teacher autonomy, relatedness, and competence?

- What are we doing to build collective teacher efficacy in our school?

- How are we supporting Teacher Agency?

- How do we ensure goal clarity and consensus at our school?

So, What Next?

I wrote this book because at the beginning of my career, I felt unprepared to be a teacher, and I wanted to share some of the lessons I had learned along the way that helped me to become a better teacher. When I look at what I have written, I think the result is much more than I had initially imagined. This book has built a compelling case that to improve teacher practice and student learning, we need to make classroom culture, which I have called classroom vibe, the focus of our improvement efforts. This focus is not just for teachers, though. There is a powerful case that school leaders need to focus on supporting teachers to do precisely this.

A great many things have been covered in this book. I have summarised the four inter-related key takeaway points below.

TEACHERS ARE IMPORTANT

There should be no doubt that teachers and the work that they do matter. The research tells us that within our schools, it is our teachers who are the most powerful lever we have to impact student learning. Teachers are then clearly important. In addition to their potential impact, we also know that the underlying motivation attracting people into the teaching profession is largely positive. As I said, no one becomes a teacher to do a lousy job. That said, through personal reflection and consideration of survey data, we also know that not all teachers are equal. Indeed, we saw how students experience and perceive teachers can vary quite dramatically. This point is important as student perceptions of teaching (as collected using student surveys) are reliable in predicting teacher impact upon learning and a great source of insight into the quality of teaching. It is my view that as teachers, it is our responsibility to seek to understand the variation of student experience that exists within our classes so that we can understand how we might improve.

CHANGE IS HARD

Creating change is challenging in education, and we considered several issues that can impede our capacity to improve teacher practice. In the first instance, while there is a long list of things that we know are effective teaching practices, it can be confusing, if not overwhelming, to know where to start. Related to this is that in education, within our schools and system, it can feel as though there is a lack of clarity regarding how we are trying to achieve improvement collectively. Indeed, this can manifest via a scattergun approach to improvement efforts by which teachers feel pushed and pulled in a myriad of seemingly competing directions.

Additionally, no matter how powerful a proposed improvement strategy or initiative is, if what it requires of teachers contradicts their beliefs and values about their role, it is unlikely to gain traction. The reason is that the messy adaptive nature of the change being implemented has often not been recognised, and a solution has simply been implemented off the shelf. You will recall that this distinction between technical and adaptive challenges is a critical problem and the misdiagnosis of adaptive challenges as technical challenges and seeking out inappropriate solutions.

Further to this, we saw that despite various systems in place to support change through teacher professional development and learning, one of the key elements often missing is the provision of quality evidence that supports teachers to understand that there was room for improvement in their practice and how to achieve this improvement. This is an issue because it is hard to help teachers overcome their cognitive biases in the absence of disconfirming evidence. Indeed, evidence is the key to breaching the perception-reality gap we all hold due to our biases.

IT'S ABOUT THE VIBE

This book introduced and defined the concept of classroom vibe as the learning-focused atmosphere within our classrooms as experienced by our students. A classroom's vibe is not just an intangible concept, rather it can be seen as the intersecting outcome of enhanced teacher credibility and teacher clarity, both known high impact umbrella influences.

The core argument of this book has been that a razor-sharp focus on improving each teacher's classroom vibe, over and above discrete strategies or initiatives, will yield teachers focused on improving what we know will enhance student learning. To do this, a teacher must focus on integrating effective behaviours and practices that will enhance their students' perceptions of their teacher credibility and clarity. These include:
- Capacity to build trusting, productive relationships.
- Competence as a leader of learning.
- Passion in the classroom.
- Presence and availability to support student learning.
- Capacity to impact upon student learning.
- Ability to organise student learning coherently.
- Introduce new learning.
- Support new learning with examples and guided practice.
- Capacity to embed a variety of assessment strategies effectively into practice.

To help teachers to do this, I have proposed that they should seek to understand and enhance their classroom vibe. Three rubrics to facilitate teachers to gain insights into their classroom vibe have been included. These rubrics support the collecton of evidence from three sources – self, peers and students. Further, I have outlined an inquiry cycle that can be used to engage in the challenging process of improvement, using evidence to identify opportunities for improvement and then engaging in an ongoing, iterative process of making small improvements to their practice. It is only through engaging in a process like this that teachers can step up to their responsibility of understanding and enhancing the vibe in their classrooms. In fact, I would say that only by using a process such as this is it truly possible to breach the perception reality gaps we all have and to overcome our cognitive biases to identify the areas of our practice for improvement that will have the greatest impact on our students' experiences and ultimately learning outcomes.

LEADERS ARE ONLY AS GOOD AS THEIR TEACHERS

Finally, the impact of school leadership through organisational culture was discussed. Three important cultural considerations for school improvement include Self Determination Theory, Collective Teacher Efficacy, and Teacher Agency. Drawing upon these three considerations, I argued that school leaders must focus their efforts on building the culture within their school, the school vibe, if you will, such that their teachers are effectively empowered to understand and enhance the vibe in each of their classrooms. With regards to school leadership, my argument is that to achieve their potential as leaders they have the responsibility to harness the maximum impact of their teachers. To do this they must focus on building the culture, the vibe, within their school such that their teachers are effectively empowered to focus their efforts on understanding and enhancing the vibe in each of their classrooms. This means creating systems, structures, and processes to emancipate teachers from distractions and that support and empower them to make changes to improve their practice by focusing on their classroom vibe. This is about empowering teachers to authentically engage in the messy adaptive that is required to re-frame ones personal theory of action and create change.

IN CONCLUSION

For teachers, we need to step up and take responsibility for the vibe that we cultivate in our classrooms. We need to seek evidence regarding the nature of our practice and then work iteratively to improve what we do.

For school leaders, we need to do everything within our power to support our teachers to enhance their classroom vibe.

I hope that you have enjoyed reading this book. I hope it has challenged your thinking, caused you to reflect on your practice, and aim to be even better.

In summing up it's the atmosphere,
it's the culture, it's the climate,
it's the community, it's the connections,
it's the vibe and, no that's it, it's the vibe. I rest my case.

Chapter Notes

INTRODUCTION

1. Five top reasons people become teachers – and why they quit. <https://www.theguardian.com/teacher-network/2015/jan/27/five-top-reasons-teachers-join-and-quit>.
2. Data from a survey of 20,000 US Public School Teachers in *Primary Sources: America's Teachers on Teaching in an Era of Change* (3rd ed.) by Scholastic Inc. and the Bill & Melinda Gates Foundation, 2014.

CHAPTER 1

3. This is an adapted quote from the Australian movie *The Castle*. In writing a book about classroom vibe I could not help myself, please forgive me.

CHAPTER 2

4. Adapted to be gender neutral from a quote attributed to Norman Vincent Peale, author of the book *Six Attitudes for Winners*.

CHAPTER 3

5. This is an adapted version of a quote from Fisher and Frey (2011); it has been amended to include the word 'ALL' drawing upon the work of Rubie-Davies (2007) and John Hattie.

6. This is an adapted version of a quote from Fisher and Frey (2011); it has been amended to include the work 'ALL' drawing upon the work of Rubie-Davies (2007) and John Hattie.

CHAPTER 4

7. This quote has been amended, the original Ausubel quote used the word 'him'.

CHAPTER 5

8. This illustration has been based on the many works of Richard Ryan and Edward Deci (i.e., Deci & Ryan, 1985; Ryan & Deci, 2000, Ryan & Deci, 2017; etc) and the countless other researchers in the field of Self-Determination Theory.

References and Suggested Reading

A great many books, articles, and web resources have been reviewed in the writing of this book. I would like to thank all the authors from whom my ideas have been derived. I am no Newton, but his quote rings true:

*If I have seen a little further,
it is by standing on the shoulders of giants.*

Ausubel, D. P. (1968). *Educational Psychology: A Cognitive View*. New York: Holt, Rinehart & Winston.
Balch, R. T. (2012). The validation of a student survey on teacher practice. (Unpublished Ph.D. thesis). Nashville, TN: Vanderbilt University.
Bandura, A. (1977). Self-efficacy: Toward a unifying theory of behavioural change. *Psychological Review*, 84(2), 191–215.
Bandura, A. (1993). Perceived self-efficacy in cognitive development and functioning. Educational Psychologist, 28(2), 117–148.
Basawapatna, A., Repenning, A., Koh, K. H. and Nickerson, H. (2013). *The Zone of Proximal Flow: Guiding Students through a Space of Computational Thinking Skills and Challenges*. ICER 2013 – Proceedings of the 2013 ACM Conference on International Computing Education Research, 67–74.
Bloom, B. S. (1968). Learning for Mastery. Instruction and Curriculum. Regional Education Laboratory for the Carolinas and Virginia, Topical Papers and Reprints.

Bloom, B. (1981). *All Our Children Learning – A Primer for Parents, Teachers, and Other Educators*. New York: McGraw-Hill.

Boynton, M., and Boynton, C. (2005). *Educator's Guide to Preventing and Solving Discipline Problems*. Alexandria, VA: Association for Supervision and Curriculum Development (ASCD).

Carroll, J. B. (1963). A Model of School Learning. *Teachers College Record*, 64(8), 723–733.

Chesebro, J. L. and McCroskey, J. C. (2001). The relationship of teacher clarity and immediacy with student state receiver apprehension, affect, and cognitive learning. *Communication Education*, 50(1), 59–68.

Christophel, D. M. (1990). The relationships among teacher immediacy behaviours, student motivation, and learning. *Communication Education*, 39(4), 323–340.

Clark, R. C., Nguyen, F. and Sweller, J. (2006). *Efficiency in Learning: Evidence-based Guidelines to Manage Cognitive Load*. San Francisco: Pfeiffer.

Clarke, S. (2019). *Moving From Product to Process Success Criteria*. Corwin. <https://corwin-connect.com/2019/06/moving-from-product-to-process-success-criteria/>.

Clarke, S. (2021). *Unlocking Learning Intentions and Success Criteria: Shifting From Product to Process Across the Disciplines*. Thousand Oaks, CA: Corwin.

Clinton, J., Hattie, J., Cairns, K., Dabrowski, A., Abrahams, T. and Brcan, S. (2014). Visionary feedback: The use of real-time captioning and teaching analytics to make teaching and learning visible. Paper presented at the 7th International Conference of Education, Research and Innovation (ICERI), Seville, Spain.

Coe, R. (2018). *What should we do about meta-analysis and effect size?*, Centre for Evaluation & Monitoring. Cambridge CEM Blog. <https://www.cem.org/blog/what-should-we-do-about-meta-analysis-and-effect-size>.

Cross, K. P. (1977). Not can, but will college teaching be improved. *New Directions for Higher Education*, 17, 1–15.

Csikszentmihalyi, M. and Csikszentmihalyi, I. (1975). *Beyond Boredom and Anxiety: The Experience of Play in Work and Games*. San Francisco: Jossey-Bass.

Csikszentmihalyi, M. (1997). *Finding Flow: The Psychology of Engagement with Everyday Life*. New York: Basic Books.

Deci, E. L. and Ryan, R. M. (1985). *Intrinsic Motivation and Self-determination in Human Behaviour*. New York: Plenum Press.

Deci, E. L. and Ryan, R. M. (2000). The 'what' and 'why' of goal pursuits: Human needs and the self-determination of behaviour. *Psychological Inquiry*, 11(4), 227–268.

Delamont, S. and Galton, M. (1986). *Inside the Secondary Classroom* (RLE Edu O) (1st ed.). Routledge. <https://doi.org/10.4324/9781315811703>.

Donohoo, J. (2017). *Collective Efficacy: How Educators' Beliefs Impact Student Learning.* Thousand Oaks, CA: Corwin.

Donohoo, J., O'Leary, T. and Hattie, J. (2020). The design and validation of the Enabling Conditions for Collective Teacher Efficacy Scale (EC-CTES). *Journal of Professional Capital and Community,* 5(2), 147–166.

Doran, G. T. (1981). There's a S.M.A.R.T. Way to Write Management's Goals and Objectives. *Management Review,* 70, 35–36.

Duckworth, A. (2016). *Grit: The Power of Passion and Perseverance.* New York: Scribner.

Dweck, C. S. (2008). *Mindset.* New York: Ballantine Books.

Erwin, J. C. (2004). *The Classroom of Choice: Giving Students What They Need and Getting What You Want.* Alexandria, VA: Association for Supervision and Curriculum Development (ASCD).

Evans, D. (2012, February 17th). *Make Them Believe in You.* [Blog post]. <https://www.tes.com/news/make-them-believe-you-0>.

Fendick, F. (1990). The Correlation Between Teacher Clarity of Communication and Student Achievement Gain: A Meta-Analysis. (Unpublished doctoral dissertation). University of Florida.

Fernandes, M. A., Wammes, J. D. and Meade, M. E. (2018). The Surprisingly Powerful Influence of Drawing on Memory. *Current Directions in Psychological Science,* 27(5), 302–308.

Fisher, C., Filby, N., Marliave, R., Cahen, L., Dishaw, M., Moore, J. and Berliner, D. (1978). *Teaching Behaviors: Academic Learning Time and Student Achievement – Final Report of Phase III-B, Beginning Teacher Evaluation Study.* San Francisco: Far West Laboratory for Educational Research and Development.

Fisher, D. and Frey, N. (2011). *The Purposeful Classroom.* Alexandria, VA: Association for Supervision and Curriculum Development (ASCD).

Fisher, D. and Frey, N. (2018). *Show & Tell: A Video Column/ Boosting Your Teacher Credibility.* Association for Supervision and Curriculum Development. <https://www.ascd.org/el/articles/boosting-your-teacher-credibility>.

Fletcher-Wood, H. (2019). *Responsive Teaching Cognitive Science and Formative Assessment in Practice.* London: Routledge.

Freire, P. (2006)[1970] The banking model of education. In Eugene F. Provenzo (ed.), pp. 105–117. *Critical Issues in Education: An Anthology of Readings.* Thousand Oaks, CA: Sage Publications.

Freeman, D. (1989). Teacher Training, Development, and Decision Making: A Model of Teaching and Related Strategies for Language Teacher Education. *TESOL Quarterly,* 23(1), 27–45.

Frey, N., Hattie, J. and Fisher, D. (2018). *Developing Assessment-Capable Visible Learners, Grades K-12: Maximizing Skill, Will, and Thrill.* Thousand Oaks, CA: Corwin.

Gentrup, S., Lorenz, G. Kristen, C. and Kogan, I. (2020). Self-fulfilling prophecies in the classroom: Teacher expectations, teacher feedback, and student achievement. *Learning and Instruction*, 66.

Gilal, F. G., Channa, N. A., Gilal, N. G., Gilal, R. G. and Shah, S. M. (2019). Association between a teacher's work passion and a student's work passion: a moderated mediation model. *Psychology Research and Behavior Management*, 12, 889–900.

Ginns, P., Martin, A. J., Durksen, T. L., Burns, E. C. and Pope, A. (2018). Personal Best (PB) goal-setting enhances arithmetical problem-solving. *Australian Educational Research*. 45, 533–551.

Gottman, J. M., Coan, J., and Swanson, C. (1998). Predicting marital happiness and stability from newlywed interactions. *Journal of Marriage and the Family*, 60, 2–22.

Griffin, P. (2017). *Assessment for Teaching* (2nd ed.). Cambridge: Cambridge University Press.

Guskey, T. R. and Pigott, T. D. (1988). Research on group-based mastery learning programs: A meta-analysis. *Journal of Educational Research*, 4 (81), 197–216.

Haskins, W. A. (2000). Ethos and pedagogical communication: Suggestions for enhancing credibility in the classroom. *Current Issues in Education* [online], 3(4). <https://cie.asu.edu/ojs/index.php/cieatasu/article/view/1616>.

Hattie, J. A. C. (2003). Teachers make a difference: What is the research evidence? Paper presented at the Building Teacher Quality: What Does the Research Tell Us? ACER Research Conference, Melbourne, Australia.

Hattie, J. (2009). *Visible Learning*. Abingdon, Oxon: Routledge.

Hattie, J. A. C. and Donoghue, G. (2016). Learning strategies: a synthesis and conceptual model. *NPJ Science of Learning 1*. <https://doi.org/10.1038/npjscilearn.2016.13>.

Hattie, J. A. C. and Timperley, H. (2007). The Power of Feedback. *Review of Educational Research*. 77 (1), 81–112.

Heifetz, R. A. and Laurie, D. L. (1997). *The Work of Leadership*. Harvard Business Review.

Heifetz, R. A. and Linsky, M. (2002). *Leadership on the Line*. Harvard Business School Press.

Hite, S. A. and Donohoo, J. (2021). *Leading Collective Efficacy: Powerful Stories of Achievement and Equity*. Thousand Oaks, CA: Corwin.

Jones, S. M., Bouffard, S. M. and Weissbourd, R. (2013). Educators' Social and Emotional Skills Vital to Learning. *Phi Delta Kappan*, 94(8), 62–65.

Kane, T. J. and Cantrell, S. (2010). *Learning about Teaching: Initial Findings from the Measures of Effective Teaching Project*. Seattle, WA: Bill and Melinda Gates Foundation. <https://docs.gatesfoundation.org/documents/preliminary-findings-research-paper.pdf>/.

Keller, M., Goetz, T., Becker, E., Morger, V. and Hensley, L. (2014). Feeling and showing: A new conceptualization of dispositional teacher enthusiasm and its relation to students' interest. Learning and Instruction, 33, 29–38.

Korp, H. (2012). 'I think I would have learnt more if they had tried to teach us more'—Performativity, learning and identities in a Swedish Transport Programme. *Ethnography and Education*, 7(1), 77–92.

Kulik, C. L., Kulik, J. A. and Bangert-Drowns, J. (1990). Effectiveness of mastery learning programs: A meta-analysis. *Review of Educational Research*, 60 (1), 265–299.

Leithwood, K., Seashore Louis K., Anderson, S. and Wahlstrom, K. (2004). *How Leadership Influences Student Learning*. Minnesota: University of Minnesota, Center for Applied Research and Educational Improvement.

Leithwood, K., Harris, A. and Hopkins, D. (2019). Seven strong claims about successful school leadership revisited. *School Leadership & Management*, 40 (1), 5–22.

MacNeil, A. J., Prater, D. L. and Busch, S. (2009). The Effects of School Culture and Climate on Student Achievement. *International Journal of Leadership in Education*, 12(1), 73–84.

Martin, A. J. (2006). Personal Bests (PBs): A proposed multidimensional model and empirical analysis. *British Journal of Educational Psychology*, 76(4), 803–825.

Martin, A. J. and Elliot, A. J. (2016). The role of personal best (PB) and dichotomous achievement goals in students' academic motivation and engagement: a longitudinal investigation, *Educational Psychology*, 36:7, 1285–1302.

Marzano, R. J. (2007). *The Art and Science of Teaching: A Comprehensive Framework for Effective Instruction*. Alexandria, VA: Association for Supervision and Curriculum Development (ASCD).

Marzano, R. J. (2011). Objectives that students understand. *Educational Leadership*, 68(8), 86–87.

McKeown, D., Mercer, T., Bugajska, K., Duffy, P. and Barker, E. (2019). The visual nonverbal memory trace is fragile when actively maintained but endures passively for tens of seconds. *Mem Cognit*. 2019. <doi:10.3758/s13421-019-01003-6>.

Mehrabian, A. (1971). *Silent Messages*. Belmont, CA: Wadsworth Publishing Company.

Mendler, A. (2014). *Why Do We Need to Learn This?* Edutopia: George Lucas Educational Foundation. Accessed 29 March 2021. <https://www.edutopia.org/blog/why-do-we-need-to-learn-this-allen-mendler>.

MET Project. (2012). *Asking students about teaching: Student perception surveys and their implementation*. Bill and Melinda Gates Foundation. Retrieved from: <http://www.metproject.org/downloads/Asking_Students_Practitioner_Brief_PDF>.

Nottingham, J. A. (2017). *The Learning Challenge: How to Guide Your Students Through the Learning Pit.* Thousand Oaks, CA: Corwin.

Nuthall, G. (2007). *Hidden Lives of Learner.* Wellington, NZ: NZCER Press.

Oettingen, G. (2014). *Rethinking Positive Thinking: Inside the New Science of Motivation.* Penguin Random House.

Paas, F., Renkl, A. and Sweller, J. (2003). Cognitive load theory and instructional design: Recent developments. *Educational Psychologist*, 38(1), 1–4.

Pashler, H., McDaniel, M., Rohrer, D. and Bjork, R. (2008). Learning Styles: Concepts and Evidence. *Psychological Science in the Public Interest.* 9(3). 105–119.

Pogue, L. and AhYun, K. (2006). The effect of teacher nonverbal immediacy and credibility on student motivation and affective learning. *Communication Education*, 55, 331–344.

Reis, H. T., Smith, S. M., Carmichael, C. L., Caprariello, P. A., Tsai, F. F., Rodrigues, A., and Maniaci, M. R. (2010). Are you happy for me? How sharing positive events with others provides personal and interpersonal benefits. *Journal of Personality and Social Psychology*, 99(2), 311–329.

Renkl, A. (2005). The worked-out examples principle in multimedia learning. In R. E. Mayer (Ed.). *The Cambridge Handbook of Multimedia Learning.* Cambridge: Cambridge University Press.

Rimm-Kaufman, S. and Sanilos, L. (2010). *Improving Students' Relationships with Teachers to Provide Essential Supports for Learning: Positive relationships can also help a student develop socially.* <https://www.apa.org/education/k12/relationships>.

Robinson, V. (2018). *Reduce Change to Increase Improvement.* Thousand Oaks, CA: Corwin.

Rocca, K. A. (2004). College student attendance: Impact of instructor immediacy and verbal aggression. *Communication Education*, 53, 185-195.

Roeser, R. W., Skinner, E., Beers, J., Jennings, P. A. (2012). Mindfulness training and teachers' professional development: An emerging area of research and practice. *Child Development Perspectives*, 6, 167–173.

Rogoff, B. (1990). *Apprenticeship in Thinking: Cognitive Development in a Social Context.* New York: Oxford University Press.

Rosenshine, B. (2012). Principles of instruction: Research-based strategies that all teachers should know. *American Educator*, 36(1), 12–39.

Rosenthal, R. and Jacobsen, L. (1968). *Pygmalion in the Classroom: Teacher Expectation and Pupils' Intellectual Development.* New York: Holt, Rinehart, and Winston.

Rubie-Davies, C. M. (2015). *Becoming a High Expectation Teacher: Raising the Bar.* Abingdon, Oxon: Routledge.

Ryan, R. M., and Deci, E. L. (2017). *Self-determination Theory: Basic Psychological Needs in Motivation, Development, and Wellness*. New York: The Guilford Press.

Sadler, D. R. (1989). Formative assessment and the design of instructional systems. *Instructional Science*, 18, 119–144.

Saltzberg, B. (2010). *Beautiful Oops!* New York: Workman Publishing Company.

Schon, B. (2018). Teacher agency and its role in raising achievement: What is it and can it be coached? Unpublished report.

Shulman, L. S. (1987). Knowledge and Teaching: Foundations of the New Reform. *Harvard Educational Review*, 57, 1–22.

Spitzer, H. F. (1939). Studies in retention. *Journal of Educational Psychology*, 30, 641–56.

Sweller, J. (1988). Cognitive load during problem solving: Effects on learning, *Cognitive Science*, 12, 257–285.

Texas Education Agency. (nd). *Guidelines for Modeling and Thinking Aloud. Texas Gateway for Online Resources*. <https://www.texasgateway.org/resource/thinking-expert-teacher-modeling-and-thinking-aloud>.

Thompson, R. A. (1998). Early sociopersonality development. In W. Damon (Series Ed.) and N. Eisenberg (Vol. Ed.). *Handbook of Child Psychology Vol. 3: Social, Emotional and Personality Development* (5th ed.), pp. 25–104. New York: Wiley.

Thweatt, K. S. (1999). The impact of teacher immediacy, teacher affinity-seeking, and teacher misbehaviors on student-perceived teacher credibility. Paper presented at the National Communication Association, Chicago, IL.

TNTP (2015). *The Mirage: Confronting the Hard Truth About Our Quest for Teacher Development*. <https://tntp.org/publications/view/the-mirage-confronting-the-truth-about-our-quest-for-teacher-development>.

Tomlison, C. A. (2017). *How to Differentiate Instruction in Academically Diverse Classrooms* (3rd ed.). Alexandria, VA: Association for Supervision and Curriculum Development (ASCD).

Valazza, G. (nd). *Professional development: teacher development and confidence*. [Blog post]. Retrieved from <https://www.onestopenglish.com/methodology-the-world-of-elt/professional-development-teacher-development-and-confidence/146473.article?adredir=1>.

van Merriënboer, J. J. G. (1997). *Training Complex Cognitive Skills: A Four-Component Instructional Design Model for Technical Training*. Englewood Cliffs, New Jersey: Educational Technology Publications.

Vygotsky, L. (1978). Zone of proximal development. *Mind in Society: The Development of Higher Psychological Processes*. Cambridge, MA: Harvard University Press.

Wiggins, G. and McTighe, J. (2005). *Understanding by Design* (expanded 2nd edition). Alexandria, VA: Association for Supervision and Curriculum Development (ASCD).

Williams Jnr, P. (2003). A passion for learning begins with a spark. *ASCD Education Update*, 45 (2). Alexandria, VA: Association for Supervision and Curriculum Development (ASCD).

Appendices

Appendix 1. Classroom Vibe – Self-Assessment Rubric

	Description	Disagree	Kind of Disagree	Kind of Agree	Agree	Strongly Agree
Teacher Credibility						
Trusting Relationships	I try to engage, connect with and support my students regularly and build healthy relationships in the classroom.					
Competence	I prepare for my classes in advance, have clear expectations for learning, and am confident in the classroom.					
Passion	I enjoy teaching my subject and try to communicate this enthusiasm to my students.					
Presence	I am available to help support my students in their learning.					
Impact	I understand the impact I have on my students' learning and help my students see their growth.					
Teacher Clarity						
Organisation	I map out and clarify the purpose of learning and how it links to past and future learning for my students. I create opportunities for reviewing what has been learned and make work appropriately challenging for all students.					
Explanation	I make sure that my students understand the language and knowledge of what is being taught, and I respond to their needs as I teach.					
Examples & Guided Practice	I use worked examples regularly throughout my teaching and incorporate opportunities for my students to practice into my lessons.					
Assessment	I make clear the purpose of assessment to my students and use assessment practice holistically as a part of my teaching.					

Appendix 2. Micro-Teaching & Observation Assessment Rubric

	Description	Disagree	Kind of Disagree	Kind of Agree	Agree	Strongly Agree
Teacher Credibility						
Trusting Relationships	The teacher engaged positively with students and created opportunities for students to interact in meaningful ways that built culture in the classroom.					
Competence	The teacher engaged in a way that communicated competence, including being confident, comfortable, and in control of the classroom.					
Passion	The teacher's passion for their subject and teaching was evident.					
Presence	The teacher was available to support the learning of their students. They were expressive, making eye contact, using students' names and inclusive language, and moving around the room to students when needed.					
Teacher Clarity						
Organisation	The teacher made the purpose of learning explicit to students. The work was appropriately challenging for all students. The teacher took time to support their students to review what has been learned.					
Explanation	The teacher tried to build student knowledge in an engaging manner. They used formative techniques while teaching to ensure students understood what was being taught, and responded as necessary.					
Examples & Guided Practice	The teacher shows students how to succeed in this class. The model worked examples and provided the opportunity for students to practise their new knowledge and skills.					
Assessment	The teacher clarified how students would be assessed in this class and used formative assessment strategies as part of their teaching.					

Appendix 3. Sample Student Perception of Teaching Questions

	Example Questions	Disagree	Kind of Disagree	Kind of Agree	Agree	Strongly Agree
Teacher Credibility						
Trusting Relationships	I feel trusted by my teacher. I feel safe coming to this class.					
Competence	I feel confident that I am learning new things in this class. I know what I am supposed to be doing in this class.					
Passion	My teacher is enthusiastic about this subject. I feel excited about learning in this class.					
Presence	My teacher is available to me to learn. My teacher moves around the room to help us.					
Teacher Clarity						
Organisation	My teacher explains the purpose of what we learn. My teacher regularly reviews what we have learned.					
Explanation	My teacher explains new ideas and concepts clearly. My teacher helps me understand the language of this subject.					
Examples & Guided Practice	My teacher shows me what I need to do to succeed. In class, we have the chance to practise what we learn.					
Assessment	I understand how I will be assessed in this class. My teacher checks what we know before moving on.					

Appendix 4. Classroom Vibe Goal Setting Template

Evidence-Informed Need
What does the evidence tell you that you need to improve next?

Goal
Express your goal as a statement.
I am committed to ...

Outcome
What are the best possible outcomes for achieving your goal?

Obstacles
What might get in the way of achieving your goal?
Express this as a series of "if ... then" statements.

Overcome
It is time to plan how you might overcome an obstacle that arises?

Appendix 6. Planning for Success Template

Goal/Vision:
Briefly summarise your improvement goal.

I am committed to improving my capacity to support students to review what has been taught.

Current Reality	Strategies / Actions	Planned Impact
Describe what the evidence is telling you.	Describe things you will start doing and stop doing.	Describe the goal state.

Appendix 7. Proposed Implementation of Classroom Vibe Inquiry Cycle

When	Steps/Description
Mid Term 1	**Target Class**
Mid-late Term 1	**Initial Diagnostic Data Collection**
Late Term 1	**Identify – Research – Establish – Plan**
Term 2 & Term 3	**Enact – Review – Refine – Re-enact**
Early Term 4	**Summative Data Collection**
Mid Term 4	**Evaluate**

www.ingramcontent.com/pod-product-compliance
Lightning Source LLC
Chambersburg PA
CBHW071629080526
44588CB00010B/1328